Email Power

How to get what you want
from every email you send

Steven Griffith

Email Power: How to Get What You Want From Every Email You Send

Cover design: George Foster, Fostercovers.com
Interior design: Nick Zelinger, NZgraphics.com

ISBN 10: 0-9770117-0-4
ISBN 13: 978-0-9-9770177-4-2

First Edition

Published in the United States of America by
Coaching Intelligence Press
P.O. Box 9873
Marina Del Rey, California 90295

Email Power™

Email Power™ is for you if you've ever experienced miscommunication in email, felt overwhelmed by not knowing how to respond, or wished you hadn't sent that email.

If you or your business are selling, negotiating, managing and/or providing services to anyone or for anything, you need *Email Power.*

This book is for:

CEOs	Managers
Executives	Customer service reps
Sales people	Entrepreneurs
Contact center agents	Students

You will learn to:

- Identify the emotion, tone, and real message of emails.
- Create trust and rapport in your email conversations.
- Identify communication styles and respond appropriately and effectively.
- Create agreement where conflict exists.
- Increase your skills to effectively respond to customers in writing.
- See things from multiple perspectives.
- Give feedback that is heard and implemented.
- Effectively negotiate through emails.

Your business will benefit by:

- Increased sales and profits.
- Increased up selling and cross selling.
- Greater customer acquisition, retention, and loyalty.
- Increased quality and speed of service to clients and customers.

You will personally benefit by:

- Feeling empowered and resourceful in your communications.
- Increasing the effectiveness and efficiency of your writing.
- Creating deeper and more connected relationships.
- Decreasing the time of your communication while improving the quality of your relationships.

Praise for *Email Power*

"Steven Griffith has broken the code for email communication and his secrets for success are in this groundbreaking book. Don't press SEND again until you've read it!"
– Allan Pease, Co-author of *Why Men Don't Listen and Women Can't Read Maps*

"I have been working in the business world for over 20 years and thought I knew everything! I started using the techniques outlined in *Email Power* immediately, even before finishing the first few chapters. It really works! I highly recommend utilizing the processes outlined in his book before your business loses another dollar!"
– Jim White, VP Human Resources Development
Vivendi Universal Games

"*Email Power* by Steven Griffith is to email correspondence as Emily Post was to etiquette. He has set a new standard on how to succeed in communicating by email and especially how to avoid making costly mistakes. And a great read, too!"
– Shelle Rose Charvet, author of *Words that Change Minds: Mastering the Language of Influence*

"Griffith's book is a treasure of ideas for coping with one our biggest challenges in customer contact centers: emails. There are many practical tips for both interpreting the customer's message and getting the job done in one email exchange. I highly recommend this book for your professional library."
– Dr. Jon Anton, Director of Benchmark Research
(the leading expert of customer service/contact centers)

"If there is one book to buy this year, this is the one. It has helped me learn how to communicate effectively through email and my business has grown exponentially."
– Matt Griffith, Senior Category Manager, uBid

"A change has occurred in the world of communication and a new response is needed. The response? Steven Griffith's book, *Email Power*. This book responds to the new demands email communication presents. I'm personally impressed with the way Steven has created this eminently practical application of NLP, and I recommend this book for anyone wanting to master these communication challenges."
– L. Michael Hall, Ph.D., author of *Figuring Out People* and
The User's Manual for the Brain

"In a world where email is such a huge part of everyday communication; where misunderstandings mean lost customers, sales and revenue, everyone needs this book – from call center agents to managers to executives. *Email Power* should be at the top of mandatory corporate budgets."
– Dr. Natalie L. Petouhoff, Hitachi Consulting

"Communication is of the highest importance in my job. Griffith's system has taken the guess work out of all of my communication. These techniques even work on the phone!"
– Anita Whited, Senior Supervisor, Los Angeles Police Department,
Emergency Response Department

"*Email Power* is a 'must read' for anyone who depends on email. In fact, its pointers [on rapport building] will enhance all types of one-on-one interactions – Internet, telephone, written, and in-person. Well written and very insightful!"
– Richard A. Wedemeyer, co-author of *In Transition* and
The Inner Edge

"Steven Griffith brings to light the invisibility of what is actually being said in email communication. This book is loaded with the information necessary to improve relationships, dramatically increase income, and actually gets you excited about sitting down and responding to email."
– John Dewey, M.A.

"Using the information in Steven Griffith's book, I have changed my emails from static and dull to animated letters that live and breathe, grab people's attention, and get results."
– Harry E. Keller, President, ParaComp, Inc.

"Steve Griffith has taken the scientific foundation of successful communication and revolutionized it to the ever-increasing superhighway of online communication. This book is a must for anyone desiring to increase their professional or personal success. Brilliant and forever useful."
– Gary De Rodriguez, CEO, Life Design International

"Every interaction is the most important. This includes my clients, my partners, my colleagues, my competitors, my family and friends. Griffith's system has given me the power to build trust and rapport immediately. It has completely transformed my email communication."
– David Sullivan, VP, Bearing Point

"*Email Power* provides useful word and phrase choices that enable you to send sensitive information sensitively. Now my parent/teacher communication is pleasant and powerful."
– Valerie Castritsis, teacher

"Because I rely more and more on technology to communicate these days, I need to quickly and most effectively gain the trust and confidence of my clients, my prospects, and my colleagues. Griffith's system is just what the doctor ordered. I now have the tools to build better relationships and get the results I want."
– Dave Olear, Vice President, Wells Fargo

"*Email Power* is a uniquely insightful glimpse into the next era of communication."
– Sam Deane, writer

"At last, a book that addresses how to electronically communicate! Steven Griffith's *Email Power* is the first direct, intelligent, and accessible book that reveals how to create trust and rapport in every email."
– Rebekah Vandenberg, Life Coach

"With many relationships starting online today, it is a must to be able to relate, connect, and have your message understood. *Email Power* is just the system to create that connection. A great book to humanize email communication."
– Maureen O'Crean, MBA and co-author of *I Am Diva, Every Woman's Guide to Outrageous Living*

"It never occurred to me before reading this book that I needed to pay attention to what and how I write emails. I have always found email communications difficult and somewhat impersonal. With *Email Power*, I am suddenly finding amazing success through my email negotiations!"
– Charles Pence, Realtor, Coldwell Banker, top 50 world producer

"In today's media world, you have to be able to communicate 24/7 and most of the time it is through email. *Email Power* is an exceptional book on how to get your message across everytime you email."
– Courtney Bullock, Emmy award-winning producer
Paramount television

"Communication, Communication, Communication! Steven Griffith's book *Email Power* has shifted my entire understanding of the power of communication. Whether I am replying to clients or Coaches by email, I have learned how to best engage and inspire each member of the team in the most efficient amount of time. Thank you, Steven Griffith for possessing the skills to write such an amazing book!"
– Mark MacDonald, President, Venice Nutrition

This book is dedicated to my mother, Shirley.
Thank you for all the sacrifices you have made for me.

Table of Contents

"The warrior's approach is to say
'yes' to life: 'yea' to it all."

~ Joseph Campbell

ACKNOWLEDGEMENTS

O ver my lifetime, many people have influenced me. Because of these great teachers, coaches and mentors, this book was made possible. Thanks, Mom, for your innumerable sacrifices and your dedication toward helping me become the man I am today. You gave me love and support the whole way. Thank you to my boxing coach, Tom Delaney, for your kindness and generosity. Your support has truly been a great contribution. To my friend and mentor, Gary De Rodriguez, you opened my eyes to the world of language and inspired me to discover and explore the possibilities. An extra "thanks" for your contribution to chapter four on *Precision Language*. Thank you, Rebekah, for your friendship, support, and ideas for this book. Jeremy, "Troll," thanks for holding the vision all these years and your constant belief in me. Maureen, thank you for your constant push and awesome early direction on this book. Dr. Pat Allen, your life's work in human relationships and language has been a great influence. My friend, Kristie, for opening your home to me while I wrote this book on the beautiful big island of Hawaii. Bols and Cybele, for your ideas, friendship, and fantastic illustrations. Laura, for your love, support, and proofreading time. Sam, thank you, too. David, for your friendship, and guiding spirit about life and awesome editing skills, you helped me make it over the finish line. To Dr. Natalie, for all your encouragement and creative ideas for the book; Nick, for your great formatting of the book; George, for your outstanding cover design; and Susan, Michael, and Steve for your awesome copywriting.

INTRODUCTION

Society is increasingly using technology to replace human relationships and enhance living through better and faster information. Yet, our ability to communicate and be understood is facing interesting challenges these days. The political and economic climate of skepticism and suspicion permeating our society is at an all-time high and trust is at an all-time low. The by-product of all this is that people are feeling overwhelmed, disconnected, and frustrated. This is expressed in the ways we communicate, most notably in the phenomenon brought about by the Internet: email.

I was sitting in my client Jeremy's office looking over his emails. He was negotiating a contract with the CEO of a large clothing company. I was hired to assist in the communication and negotiating process. The challenge: all communications were done through email. He had never met with the CEO with whom he was negotiating or even spoken to him on the phone.

Jeremy was becoming increasingly frustrated because each email he sent was creating greater distance between he and the CEO rather than aligning them more closely with their main goal: the signing of a contract. Things were quickly deteriorating and both parties were losing their patience.

I read each email and was amazed at how each had communicated right past each other. I quickly created a "how to" guide using my Language Response System™. *This system helped determine the CEO's style of communication, what he valued most, his emotional position, and what was holding him back. All this from his emails!*

Jeremy used this system and to his surprise, things began to shift. After just a few rounds of email, a contract was agreed on. The deal was finalized and both parties were happy.

> **With email communications, the normal cues found in face-to-face exchanges are absent.**

You may be wondering, "What was different?" "How did things shift so quickly?" It's simple: Using *The Language Response System*™, Jeremy was able to connect with the CEO, creating trust and rapport. For the first time, Jeremy spoke the same language as the CEO by communicating *with* him rather than *at* him.

Why should you take the time to analyze emails? I'm sure you're busy enough without having to add to what's on your plate. The fact is, though, it's simple to create successful outcomes that yield positive results and create relationships that flourish. We are in a day and age wherein we need to negotiate, be understood, and connect. And customers and clients expect it. If you want to satisfy customers, manage employees, close deals faster and more efficiently thrive in your business, you better be able to deliver. The greater your connection with someone, the easier and smoother your communications will be. To create this connection, you need to enter the world of the person or people with whom you are communicating.

The days when we communicated face to face have now been replaced by numerous digital devices, mainly email. The human touch in communication is quickly diminishing. As humans, our ultimate goal in communication is to be understood and when this happens, we feel accepted. Our most basic human instinct drives this need. Research supports this conclusion. A Ryan and Lynch study (1989) revealed that a "lack of warmth and meaningful relationships" played a significant role in the cause of heart attacks in people. Simply put, it is a biological need for people to feel understood. It stands to reason then, that if we want to be understood, we must learn how to reconnect as humans in our digital world. Email is an integral aspect of our digital technology, one of the greatest advancements in communication in our modern times.

Let's face it, people like people who are like them. We all gravitate to people who are similar to us, to whom we can relate, whom we are comfortable with, and with whom we most identify. The more we transform our email style to match our sender's email, the more comfortable they become with us and what we have to say. Negotiations go more smoothly, sales transpire more readily, there are fewer customer upsets, and customer issues are handled more quickly.

Email Power is a coaching and training method to help you create trust and rapport, reduce conversation time, and increase the quality of your relationships. Ultimately, it's to get what you want from every email you send. The foundation of this book is based on *The Language Response System*, a process for analyzing email conversations and determining the emotion, tone, and communication style of the people with whom you are corresponding – all in 60 seconds. It then teaches you how to respond to a sender using the correct language response. You learn how to enter the world of your client, customer, employee, or friend and respond in a way they can understand creating the results you desire. You can transform your relationships one message at a time and *The Language Response System* can get you there.

As you proceed through this book, relax and know that you are taking it all in on several levels, integrating all the information as you progress. When you are done, you will have the power to evaluate emails in 60 seconds. It's just like learning to ride a bike: Once you get it, you've got it for good. Enjoy the ride!

"I hear and I forget
I see and I remember
I do and I understand."
~ Confucius

1

UNDERSTANDING THE LANGUAGE OF EMAIL

"When the eyes say one thing and the tongue another, a practiced man relies on the language of the first."

~ Ralph Waldo Emerson

You've just returned from a great lunch and are feeling pumped to take on your afternoon's workload. Sitting down at your computer, you log onto the Internet and access your email. Several have come in and the client you want most to hear back from has responded to your morning email. Great! You eagerly open it and instantly freeze, your mouth drops open, your heart stops. Your client is fuming, his anger at you is so great he's decided to take his account and business elsewhere. You're in complete shock. Confusion, hurt and anger surge through your body, your stomach now in threatening turmoil. You can't believe this has happened. Your first thought is that the guy is nuts. You want to immediately write back. Your impulse to tell him off, to write him a spiteful note back is incredibly strong. But then you remember the last time you had a knee-jerk reaction, the wind goes out of your sails. Nothing feels worse than email regret, when you wish you had an "unsend" button. What do you do now? How can you recover this situation? Now's the time you wish someone had written an all-encompassing email communication manual.

In everyday occurrences the world over, an estimated 31 billion email messages are transacted every day and these numbers are expected to rise to 60 billion in 2006 (IDC, World Wide Email Usage study). In the U.S., 130 million employees send approximately 2.8 billion email messages daily. U.S. corporations receive approximately 50 million in-bound customer emails every day. In a recent survey conducted by the American Management Association, it was reported that 65% of employees polled spent up to two hours a day emailing. A full 10% spent more than four hours per day emailing. Some research suggests that 80% of business communication is now handled via email. The question becomes: How much damage is being done in these communications? How many deals are being lost? How many people are getting insulted, hurt, or angered to the point that they are no longer motivated or engaged? How many relationships have gone sour without an understanding of why?

These and many other questions are what prompted the research, training program, development, and the ultimate writing of this book. My clients, friends, and associates kept running into the same problem. It seemed that there was a critical communication issue no one had ever been able to address. With my 15 years of expertise in communication coaching, I began to see the same pattern. Time after time, the writer of the email had no idea the affect their words had on others. And when they got a response they were not expecting, they would respond exactly as they should not, making the problem exponentially worse. As I continued coaching people, I realized that if they had a system to understand the incoming email, as well as the person who wrote it, they could respond in a way that would create a favorable outcome. Over time, I created seminars, workshops, and a training company in these new methods. The results were phenomenal. I discovered I'd come up with a system that could help businesses and people to communicate better in their everyday lives, *Email Power: How to get what you want from every email you send.*

The new trend in instant messaging (IM) and text messaging within organizations is growing rapidly as well. Email has replaced how we once conducted business either face to face or via telephone. With email and instant messaging, the signaling cues of a normal face-to-face exchange are absent: eye contact, vocal cues, and body language are gone. And there is no feedback loop or way to adjust as communications develop.

> *We need to enter the world of the person or people with whom we are communicating.*

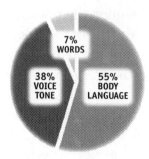

Dr. Albert Mehrabian of UCLA researched the importance of verbal and non-verbal messages in communication. In his research, he found that 93% of all communication is non-verbal: 55% is body language and 38% is voice tone. The remaining 7% is comprised of the actual content of what we're saying, the words.

With that said, Mehrabian's model is a seminal piece of research and clearly demonstrates the importance of all three channels of communication. It is important to note, though, that with any model, care must be taken when applying this to different communication situations. The percentages listed above can and do vary greatly depending upon a number of factors: The context of the communication, how much trust and rapport is already present (familiarity), how well you know the person, etc. These findings should only be used as a guide. Body language and voice tone appear to be most important when the message seems to be incongruent with one or more of the channels. In these situations, body language and voice tone become paramount in the transfer of meaning. Words, tone of voice, and body language must be consistent with and support one another. Words in many situations, especially after a degree of trust and rapport have been established, have a much greater impact than just 7 percent.

> ### *Just as individual as our finger-prints, so is our language.*

When speaking with someone in person, we intuitively know if they are being sincere or not. We have all experienced this to one degree or another. Often, we know if news is good or bad before a word is spoken. When my doctor examines my sinuses during the cold and flu season, I always know if it's good news or bad news before he even says a word, just by the look on his face.

We all do this by using non-verbal signals to determine if what we're hearing rings true for us. These non-verbal indicators are absent in email conversation, leaving the reader to decipher words with 93% of the clues missing. The very fact that we are staring at an electronic machine in and of itself begins the disconnection process. It is no wonder the misinterpretation of email messages is a daily occurrence that causes personal relationships to deteriorate and costs businesses billions of dollars in lost revenue. Consequently, we are forever scanning the emotional landscape of our emails for clues to determine what is really being said.

Since the introduction of computers, people have begun to treat others as digital beings, as an appendage of their computer. We've forgotten that there are people connected to their email addresses. As a result, we've managed to disconnect ourselves from our humanity and our shared human experience, and begun to feel that we as individuals no longer matter. We are simply conveyers of information without all the qualities of our humanness that make us engaging, compassionate, patient, respectful, etc. The time has come to reconnect to our humanness and use this extraordinary technology to create mutually beneficial relationships that honor each other's experiences and to not only solidly establish deeper levels of connection, but greater trust and rapport.

The Importance of Trust and Rapport in Conversation

We are continually checking our emotional landscape to see if it is okay to trust others and the world at large. When trust and rapport are present, we are heard, people listen, and there is comfort and ease. Do you remember being in rapport with a friend? It was easy as you both moved with elegance and timing in your conversation. You almost knew what the other person was going to say before they said it. It just felt good.

On the other hand, we all know what it is like to not trust and what it feels like to not be in rapport. Imagine a time when no matter what you said or how you said it, the person with whom you were talking just didn't get it. You felt uneasy and the communication was challenging. You were not in rapport.

Building a Record of Trust and Rapport

Each time an email conversation occurs with a client, customer or colleague, we have the opportunity to build a record of trust and rapport. It either supports or detracts from the quality of our relationship. Trust and rapport are always changing. They never stay the same. When both are high, communication is easy, fast, and effective. When both are low, communication is challenging, slow, and ineffective.

Webster's (second edition) definition of trust and rapport reads:

Trust: Assured reliance on the character, ability, strength, or truth of someone or something.

Trust creates a feeling of being safe and secure, which leads to:

Rapport: Relations marked by harmony, conformity, accord, and affinity. It is the ability to connect and relate to another person.

When these magical conditions are present, communication is simple, easy, we feel understood, and we also feel a sense of connection. Unfortunately, this is not always the case. There are times when the emails we receive are challenging.

Our Choice of Words Creates Our Reality

The English language has the greatest number of word choices: approximately 750,000. The average English-speaking person uses approximately 2,000 of those words in their vocabulary, less than .5 percent of what the English language has to offer.

When we write or speak, our word choices create a physiological response in the person with whom we are communicating- and vice versa. It is through the individual interpretation of words and phrases that feeling or emotion is created. Think of a time when you received bad news. Now think of a time when you received great news. How did that feel? In each situation it was your interpretation of the words that created the positive and negative emotion you felt. Each word we read or hear has the potential for an emotional response. For example, what emotions do you feel when you read the following three words? (Read and experience what occurs for you with each word for 5 seconds. Notice your emotional response to each word.)

> *It is through how we use language in our email that we create trust and rapport.*

- Love

- War

- Vacation

Language is the currency of our life and the words we choose shape our reality. They are the map to our beliefs, values, emotions, and personality. It is the choice and manner in which we write that gives us the clues to what is happening in our world.

There are two communication styles present in every email conversation: your's and the sender's.

All language is an attempt to persuade someone. There is no neutral language. Each word we use in our conversations and written communications has a specific intention. Our day consists of multiple conversations, all of which have various desired outcomes: to be respected, understood, agreed with, or just listened to. There is always an outcome.

We use language to get what we want, or sometimes, what we don't want. The more skilled you are with your email language, the more possibilities you can create. This gives the person with whom you are communicating clarity and the ability to make more appropriate choices.

This becomes a significant issue in business when the words and the tone we use can be the difference in closing a deal or not, of satisfying a customer or losing them, or empowering an employee or discouraging them.

In their recent book, *First Break All the Rules*, Marcus Buckingham and Curt Coffman reported some key findings in their Gallup poll study of a billion customer interviews over 20 years. They found that partnership and advice were the most significant aspects of a customer's expectations. They wrote,

> *"...to meet this expectation, you need employees on the front line who are wired to find the **right words** and **right tone for each specific customer**."*

Now that we have the Internet for high-speed communication, we need to learn how to create a human connection that compliments this speed. This applies to virtually anyone who uses email from company presidents to managers at all levels, client and customer service departments, call centers, marketing, advertising, sales, etc.

The quality of your life is in direct correlation to your ability to communicate. Since you can't "unsend" email, you might as well become a pro in your communication and get the results you want.

How We Create Our Conversation Reality

Most of us enter the world thinking everyone is like us. Then, when we have a disagreement, a difference of opinion or we just aren't understood for who we are, we wonder, "What's wrong with them?" Nothing! They just interpret and perceive the world in their way. This process of interpretation is called generalizing, deleting, and distorting? It's our process for creating meaning of the world.

Here's how it works: As information comes into our brain through our senses and in order to handle the billions of pieces of information:
- we assign information to general categories,
- delete what is not relevant, and
- distort other information to fit our model of the world
- all of this unconsciously happening in microseconds.

This process is based on our individual personal filters, which consist of beliefs, values, attitudes, memories, etc., all unique to our model of the world. The end result is an internal representation creating emotions, feelings, and thoughts. We use our language to then communicate these feelings and thoughts about our experience.

In every conversation, this process is taking place and most people are not aware that this filtering system is at work. As a result, we often don't hear or process what is really being said. We simply get in the way of ourselves. Is it any wonder there is massive miscommunication?

> *We are meaning making machines.*

Essentially, we are meaning making machines – we create our reality via the meaning we assign to things.

The following are factors that make up our own reality in conversation:
- Emotional State/Stress
- Values and beliefs
- Attitudes
- Memories
- Ethnic heritage and religion
- Education and profession
- Gender
- Economic status
- Geographic culture
- Language

Independent of these considerations, our culture and educational systems give us minimal training and skills covering how to respond when evaluating written or spoken communication. Human communication is not just a transfer of information from one person to another or one email to another. People rely on their intuition, subjectivity and emotions, which is a moment-to-moment experience.

A great real-life example of how people process information – *generalize, delete* and *distort* – involves an episode of the top-rated television show *American Idol.*

A lovely girl gave a great effort and was met with the critical eye of Simon Cowell. He told her she'd given an enthusiastic performance but that her voice was terrible. When she returned to the general holding area for the contestants, she told everyone the judges loved her and that she just needed a little work. Was she in the same reality as Simon? Apparently, she heard only what she wanted to hear.

The Challenges of Email Communication

By its very nature, email communication is a monologue with no feedback loop. In regular conversation, we can adjust our voice tone and/or body language as we proceed through our conversations. Since the feedback loop is missing in email, the reader must create the tone, which may or may not be accurate, e.g., emails that are supposed to be funny are mistakenly taken seriously and serious emails are thought to be funny. These misinterpretations begin the breakdown of trust and rapport, and a potentially costly cycle begins.

This is where *The Language Response System* becomes your most valuable asset for affecting quick and constructive analysis of incoming emails, and replying with the most appropriate and effective response that produces a win-win relationship.

Top Ten Email Challenges

1. Email lacks tone; no body language or voice tone
2. Email is a monologue
3. Email arrives instantly and creates a sense of urgency
4. Email communication is centered on the writer
5. Email communication has no feedback loop
6. Email invites a quick response
7. Email can trigger an emotional reaction

"A computer lets you make more mistakes faster than any invention in human history with the possible exception of hand guns and tequila."

~ Mitch Ratcliff

8. Email is permanent when sent
9. Email is open for misinterpretation
10. Email has the potential for exaggeration and fabrication

Email is one of the greatest advances in communication of our time. It allows 24-hour access to clients, customers, colleagues, and friends. Here is when to email and when to avoid emailing.

Email When:

- you want to deliver a message across different time zones and the information is ready when the receiver opens it,
- you want to send a message to multiple locations,
- you want to stay in contact with clients and customers,
- you want to follow up from a call or face-to-face meeting, or
- you want to document a phone or face-to-face conversation.

Avoid Email When:

- your conversation is sensitive or confidential in nature,
- your topic could easily be misunderstood or misinterpreted,
- your topic requires feedback within the conversation,
- your topic requires a fast response, or
- delivering bad news.

Email Power is organized to first teach you how to evaluate and diagnose an email and how to enter the world of the person with whom you are communicating. It then teaches you, using *The Language Response System,* how to initiate and respond to emails. Once you have identified the communication style and emotion of an email conversation, you have the ability to respond with power and persuasiveness. When you communicate in the sender's style, you're understood and get the results you're seeking. Conversely, you will also be helping the sender do the same with you. In this manner, both parties are rewarded and stand to gain greater mutual respect.

Essentially, what you are learning with *The Language Response System* is how to gather intelligence that will then help you make more informed and well-composed email communiqués. Everyone benefits when the communications they have with others connects. The intention of this methodology is not to manipulate others, rather simply provide you with tools that will connect you on deeper and more authentic levels in all your relationships. Keeping that in mind, let's move on to learning about the four types of communication styles: Visual, Auditory, Kinesthetic, and Digital. And at the end of Chapter 2, you'll have the opportunity to take a short questionnaire to determine which is your primary style of communication.

2

LEARNING TO RECOGNIZE THE COMMUNICATION STYLE OF THE SENDER

"To effectively communicate, we must realize that we are all different in the way we perceive the world and use this understanding as a guide to our communication with others."

~ Anthony Robbins

We receive information from the world around us through all of our senses: sight, hearing, touch, taste, and smell. We interpret and represent this information in our mind via a combination of sensory systems and inner dialogue. As this information enters our brain, it is coded accordingly. For example, some people receive information and code it as a picture, others as sound, and still others as an emotion/feeling. With all this incoming information, four distinct communication styles are developed.

The Four Communication Styles

Human beings communicate information in one of four styles: *Visual, Auditory, Kinesthetic,* and *Digital.* While you continue to use all four communication styles interchangeably, at some point in your development, one of these senses takes over and becomes your primary one. It is your way of creating meaning out of your experiences. By identifying the primary communication style used in emails you receive, you can respond in the style the sender will best understand.

We use the four communication styles in very distinct ways:

- **Visual (V):** how things look or what is seen.
- **Auditory (A):** how things sound or what is heard.
- **Kinesthetic (K):** how things feel.
- **Digital (D):** how information is processed in one's head and through internal dialogue.

Imagine your first day of school and your teacher begins talking in a foreign language. During the class, you strain to understand what is being said and miss the majority of what the teacher is trying to convey. This is what takes place when you write in a different communication style than the style used by the person with whom you are having an email conversation. You are literally expecting the receiver to decode the message. In this process, the meaning is lost and the real message diluted. The more you become attuned to the person with whom you're communicating, the more he or she will welcome and understand your message. You become more like them.

While each style has advantages in different contexts, no style is better than another. In addition, our communication style can change in different areas of our life. For example: A person may be Digital at work (processes things in their head) and in their private relationship may be Visual (creates meaning by how things look). In email, we can identify an individual's style by the words they use.

In this chapter, you'll learn how to identify the communication style of emails you receive and how to respond appropriately to develop rewarding and successful relationships, both in business and in your personal life.

Communication style is the context, the *how* of our communications. Our language is derived from our unconscious and is the greatest indicator of our communication style. In the world of email, the identification of a person's style creates the opportunity to respond to them in the way they communicate. By honoring their communication style, you create trust and rapport.

> *If you do not know a person's sensory system, use sensory rich language that includes each category.*

The Visual Communicator

People who are visual generally stand or sit with their heads and/or bodies erect, with their eyes up, and are well-groomed and orderly. They speak at a faster pace with bursts of expressive-ness, higher tones, and with greater volume. They process and organize their world through what they see. They tend to move quickly, memorize by seeing pictures, and are less distracted by noise. Many have trouble remembering verbal instructions because their minds tend to wander as they unconsciously continue seeking visual stimulation. A visual person is interested in how your program, your solution, your proposal, or your presentation "looks." In communication, Visuals make up the largest segment of our population.

As a reminder, these characteristics are a general guide to physical qualities and behaviors. It is important to understand that in each category, these are tendencies and not hard and fast rules. Use these descriptions strictly as guides – as observations of behavior – and not labels. Be aware that your style and other people's communication styles can and will change in different contexts.

The Visual Vocabulary

The following words and phrases are used by Visuals to communicate meaning.

Visual Word Choices

Clear	View	Imagine	Sight	Picture
Vision	See	Look	Illuminate	Clarify
Show	Read	Focus	Crystal	Highlight
Appear	Diagram	Glare	Notice	Imagine
Blind	Horizon	Envision	Glance	Dim

Visual Word Choices (continued)

Outlook	Reveal	Perspective	Blurred	Bright
Glance	Display	Sightsee	Observe	Visualize
Vanish	Preview	Expose	Faced	Vivid
Scan	Gaze	Staring	Conceal	Glimpse
Clarity	Examine	Hindsight	Fuzzy	Enlighten

Visual Phrase Choices

Can you see my...?
Let's focus on the job.
Imagine the finished product.
Look into the future.
This is my vision.
Beyond a shadow of a doubt.
A sight for sore eyes.
Horse of a different color.
Staring off into space.
Paint a picture.
Do you get the picture?
I want to make this crystal clear.
Can you picture that?
Highlight the important points.
Let's look to the future.
Will you shed some light on this?
We see eye to eye on the subject.
See you later.
Can you imagine?
He has a bright future.

In order to create rapport, it is important to respond in a similar manner. Here are some examples of Visual sentences and how to respond.

Visual Approach	Response
I am not seeing your point.	Let me show you.
This approach is not clear to me.	I will show you from this perspective.
Explain your focus.	We see two areas of interest.
I can't see how we can accomplish that.	Picture the proposal from this view.

Visual Rapport

John (Visual):	*How does the proposal look to you?*
Sue (Visual):	*It looks great.*

John (Visual):	*Looking it over, I see it being very successful.*
Sue (Visual):	*My view is the same.*

Rapport = Connection

When communication styles are different, the conversation becomes difficult to navigate and discomfort develops on both sides. Here is an example of mismatched communication styles in conversation.

Visual Mismatched Conversation

John (Visual): *How does the proposal look to you?*
Sue (Kinesthetic): *I feel it is very good.*

John (Visual): *But you don't have a clear picture of the situation.*
Sue (Kinesthetic): *I have a grasp of the entire project.*

John (Visual): *I don't see how you have enough information.*
Sue (Kinesthetic): *I feel I do.*

As you begin to evaluate email conversations, it is important to identify the primary style used by the sender and respond with the same style.

The Auditory Communicator

 Auditory people process and organize their world by how things sound and are very sensitive to sound. They enjoy conversation and listen with great intent and interest. They seem to absorb information just by listening. They do not tolerate loud or harsh sounds and tend to move a bit slower and more deliberately than do Visuals. Auditorys will ask you to repeat what you've said and have a tendency at times to dominate a conversation and talk over others – they need to be heard. They usually have a pleasantly modulated voice with good sound quality.

Auditorys, just like Visuals, use the other three communication styles as well. In communication, Auditorys create rapport by how things sound. They will be interested in your program, your solution, your proposal, or your presentation if it *sounds* right.

The Auditory Vocabulary

The following are words and phrases used by Auditorys.

Auditory Word Choices

Hear	Tell	Speak	Talk	Sounds
Voice	Question	Heard	Call	Listen
Attention	Inquire	Resonate	Tone	Loud
Remark	Silence	Shout	Undertones	Remark
Harmonize	Proclaim	Scream	Babble	Converse
Announce	Gossip	Tune	Echo	Translate
Overtones	Rumor	Noisy	Earful	Utter
Roar	Outspoken	Ask	Insult	Noisy
Yell	State	Shout	Mention	Divulge
Debate	Recite	Complain	Request	Phrase

Auditory Phrase Choices

It sounds good to me.
Tell me the process again.
Let's talk this over.
Listen to the presentation.
Do you hear me?
That really resonates with me.
Give him a call.
Keep an ear open.
Call attention to his performance.
He was completely tongue tied.
It was clear as a bell.
Give an account of.
Hold your tongue.
Loud and clear.
In a manner of speaking.
Purrs like a kitten.
Pay attention to.
Voice an opinion.
Idle talk.
Friends, Romans, lend me your ears!

Auditory Approach	Response
I want to hear the proposal again.	Let me rephrase what I said.
It does not sound right.	I'll re-tell it.
I did not hear the details.	Listen to the proposal.
Can we talk about the details?	I'll describe it in detail.
Tell me your opinion again.	It really resonates with me.

Auditory Rapport

John (Auditory):   *How does the proposal sound to you?*
Sue (Auditory):   *It sounds very good.*

John (Auditory):   *Listening to the presentation, it really resonated with me.*
Sue (Auditory):   *I hear what you are saying and I agree.*

Auditory Mismatched Conversation

John (Auditory):   *How does the proposal sound to you?*
Sue (Kinesthetic): *I feel it is very good.*

John (Auditory):   *But you haven't listened to the whole project.*
Sue (Digital):   *I have. I analyzed the entire project.*

John (Auditory):   *I don't think you heard enough.*
Sue (Visual):   *I saw the whole presentation.*

The Kinesthetic Communicator

Kinesthetics access and analyze their world through their feelings. They process, interpret, and organize their world by how it feels, taking the world in through the senses of touch, taste, feel, and smell. They use conversation to transform images, words, and sounds into feelings and attach sensations to their experiences. Kinesthetics tend to stand closer to people than Visual people do and memorize by doing or walking through something. They usually speak and move more slowly with a lower voice tone. They will be interested in your program, your solution, your proposal, or your presentation if it *feels* right.

The Kinesthetic Vocabulary

The following are words and phrases used by Kinesthetics:

Kinesthetic Word Choices

Feel	Felt	Touch	Hold	Grasp
Scrape	Walk	Stiff	Soft	Hard
Smooth	Strong	Calm	Handle	Solid
Pressure	Unravel	Dry	Push	Sharp
Heated	Concrete	Emotional	Sensitive	Tension
Thick	Tremble	Hurt	Anxiety	Hug
Break	Unfeeling	Motion	Stretch	Stress
Exciting	Irritate	Support	Bearable	Force
Grab	Scramble	Unravel	Weigh	Rub
Emotional	Grapple	Warm	Slip	Work
Foundation	Bounce	Strain	Clumsy	Contact

Kinesthetic Phrase Choices

I have a gut feeling.
I sense this is the right decision.
Let's get a handle on this.
I grasp the idea now.
This is a solid idea.
He is cool, calm, and collected.
He had a soft touch.
The plan has a smooth transition.
The presentation touched me.
Let's explore the possibilities.
I am not following you.
All washed up.
Hot head.
Get in touch with.
Know-how.
Start from scratch.
Stiff upper lip.
Pain in the neck.
Come to grips with.
Hand in hand.

Kinesthetic Approach	Response
It just doesn't feel right.	Let me give you a sense of the details.
I can't get my arms around it.	Let's walk through the steps again.
I just can't grasp the proposal.	I will give you a better feel for the details.
I feel unsure about the project.	I have a firm handle on this project.
I have a gut feeling about this.	You are certainly cool, calm, and collected.

Kinesthetic Rapport

John (Kinesthetic): *How does the proposal feel to you?*
Sue (Kinesthetic): *It is very solid.*

John (Kinesthetic): *Are you sure you have a grasp of its scope?*
Sue (Kinesthetic): *I have a good feel for all of the details.*

Kinesthetic Mismatched Conversation

John (Kinesthetic): *How does the proposal feel to you?*
Sue (Visual): *It looks fine.*

John (Kinesthetic): *But you haven't been in touch with the whole project.*
Sue (Digital): *I understand the scope of it.*

John (Kinesthetic): *I feel you don't have a handle on it.*
Sue (Visual): *I can clearly picture it.*

The Digital Communicator

The Digital communicator processes and organizes the world by how it makes sense in their head. It is important to note that they operate outside the sensory level of the Visual, Auditory, and Kinesthetic as a way of communicating rather than as an actual sensory mode. Digital communicators initially bring information in through one of their senses and quickly go into their head creating a thick filter of language between their sensory perceptions. They may speak in a monotone, appear computer like, and lack emotion. They have a method of talking to themselves in their head to process information.

This group is the most opposite of the Kinesthetic's communication style. Because of the nature of our society and the influence of and our growing dependency on technology, cell phones, the Internet and lack of face-to-face communication, it has become a fast-growing category. Digitals will be interested in your program, your solution, your proposal, or your presentation if it *makes sense in their head.* Accountants and researchers are oftentimes Digitals.

The Digital Vocabulary

The following are words and phrases are used by Digitals:

Digital Word Choices

Think	Conceive	Learn	Understand	Thought
Consider	Compute	Decide	Change	Distinct
Motivate	Perceive	Study	Ruminate	Process
Logic	Fact	Calculate	Data	Computation
Conceptualize	Empirically	Know	Doubt	Digitally
Determine	Results	Interpret	Unknown	Analyze

Digital Phrase Choices

Let me think about it in my head.
It doesn't compute.
They will consider the proposal.
What is the bottom line?
What are your thoughts on the project?
Do a complete study of the proposal.
Where is the logic in your answer?
I understand the opportunity.
Let's factor in the process.
What are your thoughts?
Interpret the data.
Review the facts.
Consider these factors.
Calculate the end results.

Digital Approach	Response
I don't understand the question.	Think about these factors.
My experience is different.	I understand your opinion.
What is the logic behind the proposal?	Consider these ideas.
I want you to consider my thoughts.	I will analyze it.

Digital Rapport in Conversation

John (Digital):   *What do you think of the proposal?*
Sue (Digital):   *I think it's very good.*

John (Digital):   *Are you sure you understand the scope?*
Sue (Digital):   *I have a good understanding of the details*
                     and I think it is great.

Digital Mismatched Conversation

John (Digital):   *What do you think of the proposal?*
Sue (Auditory):   *It sounds good.*

John (Digital):   *But you don't understand the whole project.*
Sue (Kinesthetic):   *I feel I get it.*

John (Digital):   *I don't think you have conceptualized it.*
Sue (Visual):   *I have seen the entire proposal.*

We use all four communication styles in our day-to-day conversations. One is our primary style, though we do use all four interchangeably depending on context. To create an email that really connects, simply scan the email to determine the primary style of the sender and respond using words associated with that style.

Primary Communication Styles

Visual	Auditory	Kinesthetic	Digital
Clear	Hear	Feel	Think
View	Tell	Touch	Concrete
Imagine	Speak	Hold	Learn
Sight	Talk	Grasp	Understand
Picture	Sounds	Walk	Thoughts
See	Voice	Soft	Consider
Look	Question	Smooth	Logic
Focus	Heard	Strong	Sense
Read	Listen	Calm	Decide
Highlight	Call	Handle	Process
Clarify	Inquire	Concrete	Distinct
Reveal	Tone	Dry	Study
Show	Resonate	Felt	Perceive

When you match the sender's style, you enter their world and communication flows more easily. In the evaluation of an email, if you find that the sender has used an equal mixture of two styles, e.g., Visual and Kinesthetic, respond by using both styles. The next page is an example of two styles being used in one email.

Example #1:

> Insurance center,
> I am not sure about my coverage. It **sounds** to me like I am not **seeing** this **clearly**. Will you **call** and **tell** me what the coverage is? This is really frustrating **looking** for the information in my policy.
> David

The customer, David, uses words from both the Visual and Auditory style.

Visual: *Seeing, clearly, and looking*   Auditory: *Sounds, call, tell*

> David,
> Thanks for contacting us. After **looking** over your policy, I can **tell** you that you have the proper coverage. I hope **hearing** this calms you and **clarifies** your concerns. If you have any more **questions**, please contact me.
>
> Regards,
> Shirley
> Insurance Center Representative

Review of the response:

The insurance center representative, Shirley, weaves both Visual and Auditory words into the response creating comfort for David.

Visual: *Looking, clarifies*
Auditory: *Tell, hearing, questions*

If you do not know a person's style, always mirror the language the sender is using. It is also important when you don't know a person's style to use sensory rich language from each of the four styles. This will ensure that one of the styles will engage the other person and over time, you will determine which style most appeals to them. You can then build on your communication rapport and trust.

Backtracking

One of the single most important tools for creating trust and rapport is "Backtracking." When people write about a specific situation in email, they choose words they feel are the best to describe what's occurring for them in their world. The words used have a certain comfort and connection for the sender. These words are not random or without consequence.

As we mentioned previously, the words we choose come from our unconscious and therefore have great relationship to the author. Backtracking is the process of identifying the key words you think are important to the sender and using them in your response. By mirroring their words, the sender feels a deeper connection to you and your response. You consciously and unconsciously have entered their style of communication. The more your correspondent identifies with their own style, the easier they welcome and understand your message. The use of familiar words reflects they can trust you, which builds an atmosphere of safety and security. Their brain reacts to you in a more comfortable way.

Many times, people confuse Backtracking with Paraphrasing. Although paraphrasing is a very useful tool, it creates a very different response. In paraphrasing, you repeat the other person's message and use your own words. Since you are not weaving in their exact words, this opens up the possibility for misinterpretation.

> **"The sweetest sound to anyone's ears is the sound of their own name."**
> **~ Dale Carnegie**

It is important to use moderation when weaving the sender's words into your response. By mastering this technique, you will instantly improve your communications. The following is an example of using Backtracking in an email response.

John,

It is clear to me the project needs a **team behind** it with **vision**. I can't get **behind** the project without this. Please focus on these top three **initiatives:** 1. Customer Service, 2. Reduced costs, 3. Training.

Regards,
Joe

Key words:

Behind	**Team**
Initiatives	**Vision**

Backtrack Response

Joe,

Thanks for making things clear concerning your **vision** on the project. I want to help you get **behind** a solution that looks right for you. I can help the **team** with all three **initiatives:** cost reduction, customer service, and training with the pilot program. I will call you tomorrow to follow up.

Thanks,
John

Notice how the words are woven into the response. This response will feel comfortable as it is Joe's style of communication. It will land solidly. Remember: people like people who are like them.

Example #2

> Elizabeth,
> It has been increasingly **frustrating** dealing with your tech support and I am not **satisfied**. You sold me on the customer service of your company and I need a company that can **support** their product. I need to know your company is here to **help** me.
>
> Your customer,
> Allyson

Key words:

Frustrating	**Support**
Satisfied	**Help**

Backtrack Response

> Allyson,
> I appreciate you contacting me on this and I am sorry about the **frustration** you have gone through. We are committed to **supporting** you with the **help** you require. I will look into this matter personally and will make sure that any help you require is to your **satisfaction**.
>
> Thank you,
> Elizabeth

Elizabeth used Allyson's key words and responded in a way that directly addressed the issue. Allyson will feel understood and connected with because of Elizabeth's use of Backtracking.

Now that you have become familiar with the concept of Backtracking, you can use the sender's key words to create a deep conscious and unconscious connection. The more a person identifies with their own style, the easier they welcome and understand your message.

What is Your Communication Style?

There is no right or wrong communication style. The power in communication comes from knowing your style and being able to identify the style of others. This gives you the flexibility to alter your style in order to keep the flow of communication positive and moving forward. Now, let's discover your own primary style of communication.

For each of the following questions, place a number next to each answer (a, b, c, and d).

4 = Closest to describing you
3 = Next best description
2 = Third best
1 = Least descriptive of you

1. **In everyday conversation, do you usually speak...**
    a. in a quick and fast manner?
    b. with a pleasant modulated tone?
    c. with a slower, deliberate pace?
    d. in a monotone with little change in pitch?

2. **When you study for a test, would you rather...**
    a. read notes and look at diagrams and illustrations?
    b. have someone ask you questions or repeat facts out loud?
    c. write things out on index cards and make models?
    d. scan for the facts and the data to make sense of the information?

3. **When being managed in a task, do you prefer to...**
    a. be shown what to do?
    b. have the task explained to you?
    c. walk through it?
    d. review the task in your head?

4. **I make important decisions based on...**
   a. what looks best to me.
   b. which way sounds the best.
   c. my gut level feelings.
   d. a precise review and study of the issues.

5. **To learn how a computer works, would you rather...**
   a. watch a movie about it?
   b. listen to someone explain it?
   c. get a hands-on feel for it?
   d. understand and make sense of how it works?

6. **What kind of restaurant would you rather go to?**
   a. One with a nice looking interior?
   b. One with great music?
   c. One with comfortable chairs?
   d. One that is value for money?

7. **When coached on something new, would you prefer to...**
   a. be shown how to do it?
   b. be told how to do it?
   c. be walked through it?
   d. review the information in your head?

8. **When solving a problem, do you...**
   a. make pictures in your head of different outcomes?
   b. make a few phone calls and talk to friends and experts?
   c. create a model of the problem or walk through it?
   d. organize the steps, analyze the data, and draw a well thought out conclusion?

9. **You're shopping for a car. Do you buy it according to...**
    a. what it looks like and how you will look in it?
    b. what a few people say about different models?
    c. how you feel in it and how it handles?
    d. facts you gather on performance, gas mileage, warranty, and cost?

10. **When learning something new, do you prefer to...**
    a be shown how to do it?
    b. hear the instructions?
    c. perform the activity?
    d. make sense of new facts and data?

How to Score Your Answers

Total each of the a, b, c, and d answers. The highest total determines your style. If you received the highest score for A's, your primary communication style is Visual; B's, your style is Auditory; C's, Kinesthetic; and D's, Digital.

Now that you have identified your communication style, you will begin to more easily notice the style of others, those with whom you naturally connect, and those with whom you are not in rapport. Knowing this will make it easier to shift styles and create trust and rapport in your email conversations.

✔ Checklist

1. Identify the primary communication style of the sender
2. Identify key words in order to use Backtracking in your response

Action Item

You now have your first two tools for creating powerful and successful email communications. Pick an email you have recently received and identity the sender's communication style: Visual, Auditory, Kinesthetic, or Digital (VAKD). Once determined, practice writing a response using words from their primary style, as well as using Backtracking.

IDENTIFYING THE TONE OF EMAIL CONVERSATIONS

"Use what language you will,
you can never say anything but what you are."

~ Ralph Waldo Emerson

We have introduced the context, the "how" of communications, by identifying the four communication styles (Visual, Auditory, Kinesthetic, and Digital). This chapter identifies the content or the "what" of email communications. Through the evaluation of key words and phrases, you can quickly determine the tone and the true meaning of any email.

When we are in conversation, our emotional position determines the word choices we use. The same is true in email conversations. In this chapter, you'll learn how to decode the hidden messages in email conversation. It is important to recognize specific words and phrases people use because words are the roadmaps to tone, emotion, and disposition. These key words and phrases identify the true character and intent of your sender's email.

Once identified, key words give you the power to respond persuasively and with meaning.

Words Tell the Tone

When we take a closer look and identify patterns of word use, we find indications of what a person is really thinking and feeling. Once identified, the frequency and placement of these words determine the magnitude of the tone. The strength of the prevailing tone can be determined by how many times a phrase is used or the frequency of words.

While we may want to believe we are in conscious control of our language use, quite the opposite is true. Much of our communication comes quickly and naturally to us. In reality it is our unconscious mind responding from years of repetitive mental programing.

In our conversations, as we discussed in Chapter 1, we process information to create our reality in three specific ways. We *generalize, delete,* and *distort* in order to handle the enormous amount of information coming at us. What is created from this process is "tone."

Sitting in front of our computer, we only have words on the screen. There is no voice tone, body language, or eye contact. We are left with only 7 percent of the communication. Without these other clues, the words become the map.

The following tables are a guide for determining the prevailing tone of your email conversations. As you identify these words and phrases, keep in mind the context in which they are used. The frequency and the placement will also determine the magnitude of the tone. By identifying the tone of the

> ***Words
> become
> the map***

email conversation, you will be able to respond with an effective strategy. You may need to calm a situation, create action, or motivate the sender. The four basic tones are: Imperative, Affirmative, Negative, and Tentative.

A. Imperative

Have you ever received an email and felt pressured or rushed to do something? The sender used words like *must do* or *have to*? The tone was "imperative." The sender of the email felt compelled or that they did not have a choice about something. At a deeper level, they may have felt fear of what would happen if they did not take action. The following are words to look for when the tone is Imperative.

Imperative Tone

Have to, had to	Need to
Got to	Ought to
It's time	Should do, be
Must	Supposed to
Necessary	Forced to

Example:

> John,
>
> I **have** to get the project out today. It is **necessary** that we work on this until it is complete. I will call you by the end of the day.
>
> Regards,
> Larry

B. Affirmative

When you receive an email and the following words are present: I *get to, I am* or *I will*, the prevailing tone is "affirmative." In this tone, the sender is stating a positive desire to do something. Generally, these words are used when the author has free choice and/or could receive positive benefits in some manner.

Affirmative Tone

I am	I get to
Can	It is an opportunity
Permit	It is my desire
Choose to	It's my commitment
Decide	I will
I want to	It is my choice

Example:

> Jack,
>
> **It is my desire** to implement the program. We feel **it will** benefit our sales team. **I want** to get started as soon as you can roll it out.
>
> Regards,
> Ken

C. Negative

You just received an email where *I can't, am not,* and *impossible* fill the page. The tone is "negative." This type of communication lacks flexibility or the freedom to do something. The conversation limits any further opportunity or the person is choosing not to do something – there is no way out, the person sees no options. It is important to remember that these words, as with each category, are context dependent when considering whether they are negative. (Words with "not," for our purposes, are considered negative.) When you receive an email filled with negatives, the intent is pretty clear.

Negative

Am not, Will not	Impossible
Can't, cannot	Try not to
Doesn't permit	Unable to
Don't choose to	Problem
Don't intend	

In addition to the above negative tone, there is something called "negative probability," in which words are used to describe or give an indication of what you *do not* want to happen without completely committing to being part of the outcome. (When communicating, state what you desire rather than what you don't want.) In Chapter 4, we will take a closer look at precision language and its impact. For example, Negative probabilty words would be:

Couldn't	Don't wish
Don't dare to	May not
Don't deserve	Might not
Had better not	Wouldn't
Don't let	Not likely
Don't prefer	Probably not
Don't pretend	

Example:

Brian,

The timetable **does not permit** the use of your idea. **I can't** recommend that we move forward, as it **may not** be the best solution.

Adam

D. Tentative

Have you ever received an email in which the words *maybe, proba-bly,* or *could be* were present? The tone was "tentative." The sender is showing what is probable or possible, and has not made a commit-ment. In my coaching, I always recommend that when these words are present, you treat them as if they are a "no." They usually are. These words are very lethal for keeping you out of power.

I was once in a meeting with a gentleman in which after 20 min-utes, I heard over 30 probablys and maybes. I simply asked: "So what are you committed to?" He told me exactly what he was interested in and I disregarded the rest. By asking him this question, I was able to assist him in his process to get to the bottom line. He just needed a little help. At times, it is just as important to getting to "no" if that is the true reality and answer.

Tentative

Maybe	Wish
Probably	May
Deserve	Might
Had better	Would be
Let	Could be
Prefer	Dare to
Pretend	

Example:

> Anna,
> Thanks for the invitation to the workshop. **I might** be able to make it. It sounds like it **could be** an informative marketing strategy. **Let's see** how my day goes.
>
> Regards,
> John

Invitation Phrases

We can create an opening in our communication by using phrases that invite or suggest an outcome. These phrases create an environment that is comfortable and allows information to be received without pressure. Many times, when our defenses are up, an invitation is more powerful than being told what to do. We all enjoy the power of choosing rather than the feeling of no choice. An invitation creates a feeling of free choice – and is very powerful.

Invitation Phrases

I invite you
I suggest
How about...?
What if ...?
It is a good idea
It has been suggested in the past
It is possible

Example:

Gina,
I hope your travels were successful. I **invite** you to look at the proposal from the perspective of new sales, as well as established accounts. **What if** we get together tomorrow and look at how we can integrate your ideas and mine to create a winning proposal.

Have a great day,
Steven

In many emails, words from multiple categories of tone may be present. Using this as a guide, look for the prevailing tone by the frequency of use and how these tone words are used within the context/content of the email. By doing this, you can respond powerfully with an appropriate tone.

Further Considerations on Tone

Highlighted Words, All Capitals, and Underlined Words

It is common when emotions run high and patience is thin that senders may choose this technique. Avoid this temptation. It releases a whole arena of unwanted negative emotions when interpreted, as it is considered yelling. Here is an example:

> Tim,
> <u>Please stop sending me this request for days off</u>. YOU ARE NOT GETTING THE DAY OFF. Am I making myself clear?
>
> Tom

Responding With the Correct Tone

"Our greatest freedom is to choose our attitude."

~ Victor Frankl

Now that you have the ability to quickly and accurately determine the tone of the email you've received, it is important to respond appropriately. When we focus on the reader's interests, we can then craft a message that addresses their needs, concerns, and motivations. It is then and only then that we can truly create motivating and compelling messages. With the appropriate tone, the more attentive you can be to the concerns of your customer, colleague, or friend. The more easily the message is received, the greater the results. The following are a few questions to ask to create the optimal tone and direction of your message before you respond.

- Is this a formal or informal communication?
- How does the reader view you?
- What are their motivations, needs, or perspectives?
- How will the outcome positively or negatively impact them?
- What will they gain or lose?

When we take a step back and focus on what the reader truly desires, we can authentically enter their world. By asking yourself these questions, you will structure a compelling message centered on the reader's personal interests. Doors will open and actions will be taken.

Key Words and What They Represent

Another important factor of tone is key words above and beyond the previous categories. Key words and phrases give you an indication of what a person may *value*. We previously discussed Backtracking in Chapter 2 and you know that the words we use in day-to-day conversations are the words we find comfortable. They feel right and create connection to us. The more frequently you see key words in an email, the greater the impact and comfort they have for the sender.

Nancy,
Thank you for your interest. We recognize your **teamwork** and value your **commitment**. It is awesome how quickly things are moving. We would like to develop a **team** that can go into the field and make things happen. It is our intention to build the best organization **committed** to success.

Welcome aboard.

Thank you,
Chuck

What we can see from Chuck's word choices is that *teamwork* and *commitment* hold a high value in the organization.

Here are the key words used:

Commitment
Team/Teamwork

> ***The use of familiar words creates comfort for the reader.***

Knowing these key value words, we can then use Backtracking to weave them into a response. The recipient will welcome these words as they are values familiar and comfortable to them. Remember to use moderation when replying with familiar words.

Here is Nancy's response to Chuck using Backtracking:

Chuck,
Thanks for the invitation to join the **team**. I am **committed** to the project and look forward to getting started. I know you have selected top people to work together in a synergistic **team** and I am honored to be one of them.

Thanks,
Nancy

✔ Checklist

1. Identify the primary communication style of the sender
2. Identify key words in order to use Backtracking in your response
3. Identify the prevailing tone

Action Item

You now have the skill to determine what the "tone" of an email is by identifying key words.

Identifying these components gives you the strategy to initiate and respond to your emails with even greater understanding and precision.

Review two emails and identify the *tone* by the key words used. Then write an appropriate response for each email.

4

PRECISION LANGUAGE: REVEALING & UNCOVERING THE REAL MESSAGE

*"For a man's words will always express
what is stored in his heart."*

~ Luke 6:45

The ability to uncover and understand the real message of an email gives you the highest level of intelligence gathering, results, and persuasion. This chapter puts you in control when the presenting email is challenging and reconnects you to personal power.

You now have learned how to identify the tone of an email through the use of key words and phrases. In this chapter, we will take you deeper into the structure of how we *generalize, delete,* and *distort* in email conversation. Through sentence structure and content, you'll analyze at a deeper level what a person is really thinking and feeling.

At times, the true meaning of an email is not as obvious as a specific word or phrase. In these situations, specific questions need to be asked of yourself and/or of the sender to uncover the true meaning. Once determined, *trust* and *rapport* can be created through precision language. Remember: without body language and voice tone, we only have words to create that connection. The greater the precision in your language use, the greater your ability to determine the outcome. When your conversation is vague and ambiguous, you are asking the reader to guess your intent. The specifics of your conversation give you greater power for getting your point across.

Understanding a person's word usage gives you the edge.

"The most important thing
in communication is to hear
what isn't being said."
~ Peter F. Drucker

The Language of Exaggeration

In the language of exaggeration, the sender creates vagueness by omitting personal and specific information. In using exaggeration, the sender disconnects himself in order to be in a non-personal position that allows him to avoid feeling and connection.

The following are examples of the language of exaggeration.

Exaggeration	Reconnect Response Question
Everyone	Who? Who specifically?
Everything	What? What specifically?
Always	When? When specifically?
Every time and Never	When? When specifically?
Customers make this job difficult	Which customers are making this difficult?
Nancy needs to improve the use of her creative time.	How exactly?

Vagueness with Exaggeration	Upgraded Response with Specific Language
He always gives me a hard time.	Jack disagreed with me today.
The reports are always wrong.	The sales report is not balanced.
They never get it right.	The marketing department made an error.
The sales department doesn't let you make a decision.	Tom is making the decision on that account.

Each of these examples requires the reader to ask several questions. Each situation will require that you ask the sender directly or ask yourself the question about the sender. These questions bring the situation back to reality so you can move into a position of empowerment and persuasion in your email conversation. Reconnect the speaker by asking: Who or what exactly? How exactly? Specify which exactly?

These questions will help you find a solution and gain clarity for both parties. Many times, you will have to assist the sender by helping him or her return to reality. By using these reconnecting questions, we neutralize, calm, and control the situation. Follow the same procedure for each of the following categories: pronouns, verbs, possibility and impossibility, and mind reading.

The Language of Pronouns

The utilization of excessive pronouns in our language omits and generalizes the personal connection to people, places, and things in our lives. The more specific you are with your conversation, the greater understanding you can provide the reader.

The following are pronouns that create vagueness:

Pronouns (vague)	Reconnect Response
They	Who specifically?
Them	Who specifically?
He/Him	Who specifically?
She/Her	Who specifically?
It	What/Who specifically?
Those	What/Who specifically?

Pronoun Use	Upgraded Response with Specific Language
They have always been like that.	My supervisor has been abrupt in the past.
It will get the results I desire.	My sales will reach 500 this month.
I have respect for them.	I have respect for the marketing team.
Those customers are trouble.	The ABC account is late on the March statement.

Pronoun Use – Associated or Dissociated

Taking the concept of pronouns further, how a person uses them can determine their connection or responsibility in their email. Pronoun use creates one of two conditions: associated or dissociated. By identifying the pronouns used, you can quickly determine if the sender is being accountable or disconnecting themselves from the situation. Are they centered on themselves, the team, or the event? The "position" of speaking will give you an indication of where they stand.

Associated: In the following email examples, you will find the author accountable, responsible, or connected to what is happening in the email. Pronouns you'll recognize are *I, me,* and *my.* These words will give you a clear indication of the sender's connection.

Associated Words:

> I
> Me
> My
> Mine

Example:

> John,
>
> **I** have been evaluating what took place in the meeting. **I** think that **my** actions could have contributed to the outcome.
>
> Regards,
> Tom

In this email, by using the word "I" and "my," Tom takes responsibility for the outcome of the meeting. It is very clear that he is the cause of the situation.

Dissociated: this type of email creates distance between the author and the situation by using pronouns such as: *you, she, them, they,* and *him*. When the author uses these words, he is disconnecting from the situation and any accountability. When you identify the dissociated condition, it gives you a greater ability to respond appropriately.

Dissociated Words

You	Your
She	Them
He	They
Her	Their
Him	

Example 1:

John,
After reviewing the meeting, **she** is totally irresponsible. **She** must think we're stupid. **Her** comments didn't help the meeting at all.

Regards,
Tom

Tom disconnects from responsibility by using the pronouns: *she* and *her*.

Example 2:

John,
They just did not get it in the meeting. It's all about **them** and what **they** want. The focus should be on the team.

Regards,
Tom

Tom disconnects by using the words *they* and *them*. By doing this, he takes the focus off himself and puts it on the proverbial "them."

By simply changing pronoun use in an email, you can see the profound shift in the emotion and accountability of the sender. By identifying these words, you will have a deeper knowledge of how the author is operating and feeling, and how best to respond.

Verbs of Necessity and Possibility

Verbs create the action in our language and are another indicator of what emotion is present with the sender. Verbs of necessity and possibility give you a clear indication of how the author may be thinking or feeling.

Necessity

When the sender of an email uses *should* or *have to* in their correspondence, they are operating out of "necessity."

The word "should" is used when one person is blaming another or is under stress. In this way, the author can externalize their frustration or anger at a person or situation, and at the same time exclude themselves from having any responsibility. The result of using the word "should" is that the author may feel they have no choice in the matter at hand. These words provide a deeper understanding of which emotion is actually present. This knowledge gives you superior resource when considering how best to respond. The following table illustrates words of necessity and the question that will reconnect to the real meaning.

Words of Necessity	Reconnecting Question
I have to	What if you did not?
I should	What if you did not?
I must	What if you did not?

Reconnect the sender by asking: "What would happen if you did not?" This question reorients the sender to other options and creates an opening for something else to be expressed or developed other than what they are currently experiencing. Remember: their words are a representation of the emotion they are feeling inside. Each conversation's content will give you the clues to either ask yourself or the sender the reconnecting question. You are assisting them and yourself in getting to the real message. It puts you back in charge.

Example:

> Lisa,
>
> I **have to** meet with the marketing department. It is something I **should** do but it really is not my job.
>
> Diane

The sender, Diane, demonstrates how she is operating out of necessity by using the following words: *have to* and *should*. This indicates her feeling of no choice. By knowing this, you now have the power to find out what is going on for the sender and properly respond by asking the appropriate reconnecting question.

Possibility or Impossibility

When the sender of an email creates negative limitation in a situation, you will see see words or phrases such as *can/cannot, possible/impossible, what is/is not,* or *can be done/cannot be done.* They define the author's model of the world in what they see as possible and or impossible. These verbs of negative limitation are stronger than the verbs of necessity as they reduce the world to black and white. The author perceives something to be outside their ability to change or beyond their influence to make a difference. They are resigned to having no control or choice in the matter before them. The following words are key indications of what deeper emotions are present.

Words of Possibility	Reconnecting Question
I cannot.	What prevents you?
It's impossible.	What would happen if you did?

Depending on the situation, reconnect the author or yourself by asking: "What prevents me?" or "What would happen if you did?" These questions reconnect you or the sender to additional options, creates openings for new possibilities, and brings them or you back to reality.

Example:

> Dean,
> These sales figures are **impossible**. The company wants too much from me. I **cannot** make these numbers this quarter.
>
> Stephanie

Stephanie demonstrates what her emotional position is and what she feels is possible by her use of the following words: *impossible* and *cannot*. By knowing this, you can determine Stephanie's limiting beliefs.

By asking the sender or yourself reconnecting questions, you gather powerful intelligence to appropriately respond.

Cause and Effect

When the sender attributes their emotions to someone else's behavior, they create an erroneous "cause and effect" situation. In this type of communication, the sender feels as if they have no control because their internal/emotional state is dependent on the actions of another. Cause and effect occurs by making a link between one's experience and their response to an external stimulus not connected to one's self.

Cause and Effect	Reconnecting Question
He hurts me.	How does he hurt you?
Their anger makes me upset.	How specifically does it make you feel?
I feel good for making her laugh.	How did you make her laugh?

Reconnect the sender by asking: "How, specifically, do you know?" or "How, specifically, does _____ cause you to feel?"

Mind Reading

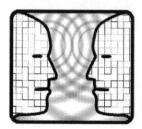 When the sender presumes to know what another person is thinking or feeling without direct experience or proof, it is called "mind reading." It may be the person's intuition or total fantasy, which is something human beings often do in their communications.

There are two forms of mind reading: (1) presuming to know what another person is thinking or feeling, and (2) assuming someone knows what you are thinking without telling them.

If someone says, "He is unhappy," "She didn't like the present I gave her," or "I know what makes him tick," you can reconnect the conversation by discovering the source and reason behind their statement. Ask how they know that he is unhappy, she didn't like the present, or what makes him tick.

Mind Reading	Reconnecting Responses
He is unhappy.	How do you know?
She did not like the present.	How do you know?
I know what makes him tick.	How do you know?

Language Without Outcome and Specifics

Conversations without outcomes and specifics create vague and ambiguous worlds with no boundaries or clear expectations.

Non-specific Language	Reconnect Question
Change my relationship.	From what into what? State your outcome or higher vision for the relationship.
Make more sales.	How much specifically? By when and how?
Reach my goals.	Define outcome. By when? How?

Ask these questions to reconnect "How," "By when," and "From what to what?" These will connect you to the specifics of the desired outcome.

Disempowering Language

"I wish people who had trouble communicating would just shut up."

~ Tom Lehrer

Your word choices in email turn your personal power volume up or down. When you use words that are disempowering, you reflect doubt and negate potential positive results. The more specific you are in an email, the greater the connection and results you create.

The following table provides examples of disempowering language and the upgraded language response.

Disempowering Language	Upgrade Response
Maybe	Yes, no, I will consider
Try	I will
Problem	Challenge
Probably	Yes, no, I will or will not
I should	I will
Kind of	It is or it isn't
You make me	I choose or I create for myself
Will you?	My request is
I don't know	I choose to know, I'll find out
It's hard	It's a challenge
I need	I desire... or I choose...

Disempowering Language	Upgrade Response
I'm not	I am
Let me	(Permission from whom?)
It's like	It is or it isn't
Do you know?	I know
I think so	I know
I want	My choice is, I require...
I must	I will, I choose
I hope	My choice is...
I've got to	I choose to
Almost	It is or it isn't
Decide	My choice is...
I would	I will
I could	I can
I wish	I choose to
If all else fails	My highest choice is...
At least	At most
Doesn't it?	Does it?
Can't you?	Can you?
Perhaps	I will, I choose
But	And

An Example of Disempowering Language

Candice,
I think **I might** need your help. **Maybe,** when you are not too busy, you could call. **I'm not sure** what your schedule is, **but** the project is due on Friday. **If all else fails,** I will **probably** work late each night. Let me know.

Thanks,
Anna

Upgraded Language

Candice,
Good morning. The project I am working on is taking more time than expected. Are you available to assist me this week? Let me know.

Thanks,
Anna

Every time you write, you are attempting to persuade someone to either do or not do something. We are in constant pursuit to get what we want. Much of it boils down to the fact that we all want to be heard, to be liked, or just understood – an intrinsic part of our humanness. The more skilled you are with language, the more possibilities you can create and the greater connections you will encourage with family, acquaintances, friends, clients, and those with whom you work. There is always an outcome for the language you use. The more attuned you are to how authentic communications build relationships, the more satisfying your life can be.

✔ Checklist

1. Identify the primary communication style of the sender
2. Identify key words in order to use Backtracking in your response
3. Identify the prevailing tone
4. Check for generalizing, deleting, distorting language

Action Item

Now that you have the tools to determine how the sender can generalize, delete and distort communication, review two emails and determine if the sender is demonstrating mind reading, cause and effect, necessity/possibility, and/or disempowering language.

Before we continue, the following story illustrates the importance of email communication in a way that is stranger than fiction. Keep in mind what we've just covered: primary communication styles, key words, the prevailing tone and generalizing, deleting, and distorting language. Follow the trajectory of this communication as it spirals into something it shouldn't have.

In early 2006, a young Boston attorney Dianna A. who had just passed the bar, emailed a prospective employer, William K.

From: Dianna A.
Sent: Friday, February 03, 2006 9:23 PM
To: William K.
Subject: Thank you

Dear Attorney K.,
At this time, I am writing to inform you that I will not be accepting your offer. After careful consideration, I have come to the conclusion that the pay you are offering would neither fulfill me nor support the lifestyle I am living in light of the work I would be doing for you. I have decided instead to work for myself, and reap 100% of the benefits that I sew.
Thank you for the interviews.
– Dianna A.

From: William K.
To: Dianna A.
Sent: Monday, February 06, 2006 12:15 PM
Subject: RE: Thank you

Dianna,
Given that you had two interviews, were offered and accepted the job (indeed, you had a definite start date), I am surprised that you chose an email and a 9:30 PM voicemail message to convey this information to me. It smacks of immaturity and is quite unprofessional. Indeed, I did rely upon your acceptance by ordering stationary and business cards with your name, reformatting a computer and setting up both internal and external emails for you here at the office. While I do not quarrel with your reasoning, I am

extremely disappointed in the way this played out. I sincerely wish you the best of luck in your future endeavors.
– Will K.

From: Dianna A.
Sent: Monday, February 06, 2006 4:01 PM
To: William K.
Subject: Re: Thank you

A real lawyer would have put the contract into writing and not exercised any such reliance until he did so. Again, thank you.

From: William K.
To: Dianna A.
Sent: Monday, February 06, 2006 4:18 PM
Subject: RE: Thank you

Thank you for the refresher course on contracts. This is not a bar exam question. You need to realize that this is a very small legal community, especially the criminal defense bar. Do you really want to start pissing off more experienced lawyers at this early stage of your career?

From: Dianna A.
Sent: Monday, February 06, 2006 4:29 PM
To: William K.
Subject: Re: Thank you

bla bla bla

Enough said. Now, let's learn about creating agreement in email, offset words, and some additional tools that will set you on a clear path to successful communication.

5

CREATING AGREEMENT IN EMAIL

"When dealing with people, remember you are not dealing with creatures of logic, but creatures of emotion."

~ Dale Carnegie

When we are experiencing "rapport" in conversation, the natural flow of information back and forth is easy and comfortable. From an early age, we are trained to use certain words when delivering unpleasant news or arguing our point of view. These words are called "Offset Words," and they break trust and rapport. The two most common Offset Words are *but* and *however*. These words negate and discount what was previously said or written, and they usually bring bad news. They create a deep internal environment that is unstable and opposing.

Do you remember someone giving you a compliment like, "Your hair looks nice, but it's really short now"? Did you really believe the compliment? Here is another example: Mr. & Mrs. Smith apply for a loan at their local bank. The bank officer sits them down and says, "Thanks for filling out the application, but...." As soon as you hear the word "but," you know what is about to be said is going to be negative, which is that the bank can't approve their loan. We are conditioned to expect bad or opposing news when we hear or read the *"but"* word.

The following are Offset Words:

Offset Words

But
However
Nonetheless
Nevertheless
Yet

Examples of Offset Words in Use

Example one: *I really enjoyed your product. It is very interesting,* ***but*** *I'm not sure we can use it.*

Real message: They are not interested. The first statement dilutes the communication: *They don't want to move forward.*

Example two: *It is a great opportunity for our business,* ***however,*** *it is a very new and unproven product.*

Real message: They are not ready.

What is this next person really communicating?

Example three: *I really enjoyed the sales training,* ***but*** *the segments were too long. The first section was motivating. John did a great job speaking,* ***but*** *it lost its impact after a while.*

When reviewing this conversation, it is noticeably incongruent: we are not sure what the true message is. The positive phrases: *I really enjoyed, was really motivating, John did a great job speaking* – are offset by negating statements: *Segments were too long, lost its impact.*

The message is incongruent and creates misdirection of the true meaning. The use of these words over time creates an internal environment that is uncomfortable and untrustworthy.

It is important to identify Offset Words, which will allow you to decode the real message and recognize the incongruent communication in the email you are receiving. Identifying the statements before and after Offset Words will give you valuable knowledge for appropriately responding to the true meaning.

> ***The unconscious mind always wants to tell the truth.***

Using Offset Words creates distrust of the entire message. At a gut level, we feel uneasy and think something is not right. It disempowers the sender because the receiver is left wondering what the real message is.

What's the Cost?

Offset Words are used to cloak, smooth over, or soften the delivery of bad news. When you are not clear, multiple emails are needed to clarify the situation. The result is a growing distrust and decreased rapport in the relationship. Time and money are the true cost of broken trust and rapport.

"The only people that listen to both sides of a family argument are the neighbors."

~ Unknown

How to Have Your Point Understood

Our conversations either create trust and rapport or they destroy it.

When you want your point heard, just add the word "and." "And" allows both statements to stand on their own. "And" creates an easy connection where both statements are heard and it allows a discussion to take place rather than an argument.

To alter the offset condition in an email conversation, you replace the Offset Word with *"and"* any place you choose to have your position heard. The use of *"and"* provides a seamless communication linking two opposing components of the conversation together. The result is no internal resistance. The conversation flows right into the other person's thought, idea, view, or feeling. They actually hear what you have to say *and* incorporate your idea, thought, or opinion with theirs.

Here's an example: I was on a vacation to the beautiful countryside of Florence, Italy. On this trip, there were friends and associates from different parts of the world. During the course of the trip, I engaged in various conversations on many topics. Toward the end of the trip, one of the guests, a television commentator by trade, said to me, "It's funny, I noticed you never disagree with me." I said, "That's interesting, I have been disagreeing with you the entire trip." I quickly referred him to previous topics and conversations we'd had over the preceding days. In review and to his amazement he said, "You know, you're right. It seemed like you were agreeing. What happened?"

I simply listened and responded with "and" when I had an alternative viewpoint. It's that easy.

Use the conjunction *and* to maintain rapport. For example:

- *"Jane, the proposal was great **and** let's add more data."*

- *"Bob, the sales report is good **and** we require it by Friday."*

- *"Larry, your sales performance is on track **and** we need improvement next month."*

Using *and* gives the person the opportunity to receive the information that otherwise would be met with resistance or not heard at all. You create an opening for the receiver to have choice in how they will respond to the matter at hand.

"Tact is the art of making a point without making an enemy."

~ Anonymous

How to Create Agreement in Email Conflict

You have just received an emotional email from a customer, colleague or friend that is blaming, argumentative, and downright nasty. What do you do?

As the topic of a conversation becomes controversial, we disagree or become emotional – our internal physiology changes and so does our language. Can you remember a time when you were arguing your point on a topic or just had a difference of opinion? What was the inflection and tonality of your words? What words did you use to get your point across? What happened to your internal state: Did your heart start beating faster? Did the blood drain from your face? Did you break out in a sweat?

The very tool we think is assisting us in having our opinion heard is actually silencing us.

For the most part, we are not truly listening to the other person, we are waiting to speak. We are preparing our remarks in our mind and we listen less. When we finally speak, we start using specific words to highlight our opposing position.

We are taught to use certain words to have our point heard: Offset Words. The use of "and" in these situations becomes even more important because of our internal environment, which is one of stress. Internally, these words shift the listening to *conflict*. We begin to fight with our words, smashing them into each other. It puts us back on our heels and we oppose the information coming at us at an even greater level. We internally protect ourselves and shut ourselves off from hearing the content. Each time a person hears an Offset Word, they resist and fight.

There is a solution – the Agreement Frame.

"We can be right or we can be happy."

~ A Course in Miracles

The Agreement Frame

When emotions run high and we choose to neutralize conflict, we use the "agreement frame" to break through the conflict. It assists in neutralizing an opposing position in email. The following are examples of how to use the agreement frame to diffuse conflict and restore trust and rapport.

Neutralize	Calm	Control
I appreciate your	Views	and...
I respect your	Saying	
(I agree that for you, your)	Feelings	
	Thoughts	

Step 1: Neutralize the situation in the email by choosing one of these phrases to create agreement with the other person: *I appreciate, I respect,* or *I agree.* This step stops the emotions from growing more intense.

Step 2: Calm the situation with a choice of words that fit the conversation. For example, you can choose from phrases like: *I appreciate your...* (opinion, thought, view, or feeling). "I appreciate your thoughts on the matter." "I respect your view."

Step 3: Take control of the conversation with the word "and."

Bill: *I think your choice of product is wrong.*
Joe: *I **appreciate** your opinion on my choice **and** I see
        a different opportunity.*

Bill: *But they're just not the right company.*
Joe: *I **respect** your position **and** I feel they're the right fit.*

Bill: *It's going to break down.*
Joe: *I **agree** from your perspective it could break down
        and I believe the company and product are solid.*

Bill: *Okay, I can see you're very sure about them.*

Joe continued to use the agreement frame until Bill could actually listen to what he was communicating. Be committed to the agreement frame. Having to use the frame a few times to neutralize a situation is common. The agreement frame provides time for the emotions to dissipate and for the other person to clear their thoughts.

In my trainings, I always do a live demonstration on the agreement frame. I pick the best sales producer or talker in the group: you know the one, the one who loves to argue. In this demonstration, we have opposing opinions on a topic and I instruct the participant to argue his side to me. The average time of this conversation is usually under a minute. That's right, under a minute! After a few rounds of the agreement frame, the confrontation is greatly diminished and they shift their focus to a more amiable dialogue.

Have you ever tried to argue with someone who is agreeing with you? It feels a little funny. When you use this frame in email, remember that you are agreeing, appreciating, and respecting their opinion, not the content. It may occur to them that you are agreeing with them. It is the neurological shift that calms the situation – they don't have any opposition, so why be defensive or argumentative? When the environment becomes calm, your content is heard.

The Agreement Frame

I appreciate your...	Opinion, thought, view...and...
I respect your...	Position, background, view, feelings...and...
I agree...for you	It looks, it feels, it sounds...and...

Giving Feedback in Email Conversation

Providing feedback can be a challenging proposition in any situation. In email conversation, it can be even trickier. The "Email Sandwich" is a process of delivering feedback that allows for the person to hear, understand, and accept the information without challenge.

Here are the Steps:

Step 1: Acknowledge the person with affirming and supportive statements ABOUT THEIR ACTIONS. This allows an opening, and honors the person. It creates a pathway for the challenging information to be delivered.

Step 2: Address the situation, problem, or concern in a direct and open way, i.e., this is the challenge; then state the facts.

Step 3: Close with another affirming positive statement. This leaves the person in a position of possibility and motivation.

> John,
> **(Step 1)** You have really done an excellent job improving your sales in the last two weeks.
> **And...**
>
> **(Step 2)** The challenge I see is your follow up with key clients after the sale is complete. Let's create a strategy for you to improve that aspect.
>
> **(Step 3)** Overall your enthusiasm and commitment at work has been great. Keep it up!

Providing feedback in any situation can be challenging. Using the Email Sandwich, you can create an appropriate atmosphere for the critical information to be understood and suitable action suggested or taken. Those difficult and touchy topics can now be handled in a way that provides possibility for the receiver and keeps the dialogue open.

✔ Checklist

1. Identify the primary communication style of the sender
2. Identify key words in order to use Backtracking in your response
3. Identify the prevailing tone
4. Check for generalizing, deleting, distorting language
5. Identify Offset Words

Action Item

Look through your previous emails and identify any Offset Words. Once you've identified them, determine the real message of the communication. Practice writing an email Feedback Sandwich response with an email you could have responded to more effectively.

6

ADDITIONAL TOOLS FOR SUCCESSFUL EMAIL OUTCOMES

"The best way to keep from stepping on the other fel-low's toes is to put yourself in his shoes."

~ Unknown

A crucial and vital position in responding to the content of any email message is remaining neutral. It's easy to make judgments and have opinions, especially when the content is sensitive in nature or has an emotional connection. Remember, you are at a disadvantage. You have no body language or voice tone clues. Giving people the benefit of the doubt is an old adage that is a must when responding to emails. You simply take the position that you may be incorrect on your assumption and/or do not have all the facts. You give the other person the "benefit of the doubt."

Benefit of the Doubt

It is easy to let the emotion of the day affect your email responses. Keep from putting your foot in your mouth by giving others the benefit of the doubt. This position keeps communication calm and respectful and allows you to gather more information before you respond, which could create conflict. Taking the time to gather the facts and get clear will save you time and aggravation, especially compared to the many conversations you will need to have if you respond inappropriately.

Using this technique gives you the ability to have all the available information you need so you can respond powerfully the first time. Going through this process is more than an effective damage control tool – it avoids the need for damage control altogether.

Have you ever been in situations where you misinterpreted a message and guessed wrong? What did it cost you? Here are some examples showing what happens when "benefit of the doubt" is not employed.

Example One

John sends this email to his team member at work.

> Jim,
> The project completion date is this Friday. Why haven't I heard back from you? What's going on with the project! The schedule better be on track – the client is getting very anxious.
>
> Regards,
> John

John is unhappy and frustrated that he has not heard back from Jim. Jim reads John's email and is very annoyed at John's tone. The tension is rising and the cycle of miscommunication begins.

What really happened? Jim's laptop was down and he never received John's first email. It's as simple as that.

Cost of the Miscommunication

John did not give Jim the benefit of the doubt and reacted before finding out more information. Now they will require a conversation or two to calm the waters and rebuild their trust and rapport with one another.

Example Two

Cindy emails her client Lisa.

> Lisa,
> I received your phone message that you needed to alter your last order. As you know, there is a 15% charge for any alterations. In the future, please make any changes in the first 30 days when there is no charge. Let me know what you would like to do.
> Thank you,
> Cindy

Lisa receives this email and is ready to cancel her entire order. She's had a bad day plus a headache when she reads the email.

What Really Happened?

Lisa left a phone message and was in a hurry. She did not leave the details of the change. She just wanted to change her address. There is no charge for changing a shipping address. Lisa is angry about the conclusion and the quickness to charge her another 15 percent.

Cost of Miscommunication

Cindy will have to have one, two, or three conversations to recreate trust and rapport so Lisa does not cancel her order.

Steps to Using the Benefit of the Doubt

Step 1: Identify any vague or unclear information and any place in the content that is creating an emotional response for you before jumping to a conclusion.

Step 2: Find out more information about the situation. Ask questions, request additional information, and gather data about what is unclear. If needed, make a call or have a face-to-face conversation.

Step 3: Re-evaluate your position with the new information, then respond.

Three Positions of Power

"We don't see things as they are;
we see things as we are."

~ Anais Nin

Now that you know how important and easy it is to employ "benefit of the doubt," here is the next step toward having the greatest insight to respond with power and persuasion.

It is well known that the best negotiators are able to experience a given situation from many different views. Their ability to move into different perspectives provides insight and clarity. There are three positions that provide this clarity.

The "Three Positions of Power" is a simple and easy tool that takes just a few minutes to master and will yield great rewards for you. When you are responding to an email, you have certain motivations, self-interests, and emotions that connect you to the conversation. It is common to get stuck in how things occur in our world and can blind you to the feelings and emotions of the person with whom you are communicating. We tend to think we are right or have a desire to be right.

The Three Positions of Power loosens your grip on the stance you take, so you can see multiple points of view. By doing this, you gain greater insight and flexibility to respond in the conversation.

Position One: Your Position. This creates the first position: *your* reality. It consists of what you think, feel, see, interpret, are motivated by, value, and want as an outcome.

Position Two: Their position. The second position is putting yourself in the shoes of the person with whom you are in conversation, i.e., what they think, feel, see, interpret, are motivated by, or value.

The second position takes some practice, so be patient. It is the place most people never want to go. Be patient, relax, and go for it.

Position Three: Neutral Observer. The third position is an imagined one, as if someone neutral was positioned outside the conversation observing. How would they view this situation?

As you move through each position, you gain clarity, which creates power, insight, and flexibility in your response. The more insight you have in a conversation, the more power you have in responding!

Now, let's go through the process.

Step 1. Stand in your shoes. Identify your own emotions, thoughts, and opinions about the email you just read and ask yourself these questions:

> What is my motivation?
> What is my outcome?
> How do I feel?
> What do I want?
> What do I value?
> What is important about this to me?
> How do I see, hear, feel, think about...?

Step 2. Stand in their shoes. Imagine the person you are writing to and create a holographic picture of them. Now, just float right into their shoes. That's right, float into their shoes.

> See what they see.
> Hear what they hear.
> Feel what they feel.
> Think their thoughts.
> What motivates them?
> What do they value?
> What are their outcomes?

This step will provide powerful insight that you cannot attain in your own shoes. No matter how out-of-this-world someone's behavior seems to be, if you are in their shoes, you will have the ability to better understand their perspective. It also allows you to connect to them in a way that relates to the emotion behind their behavior.

Step 3. Be the observer. Step outside of the conversation as if you are a neutral third party and view the conversation. In this position, evaluate what is going on. What do you see as you watch yourself and the other person?

Being the observer allows you to see the big picture from which new insight and learning take place.

Step 4. Re-evaluate the message. After moving into the second and third positions, you can now re-evaluate with new insight and determine how things "could be." Remember: any scenario you create is only real because you say so. Process the new information and take a fresh look at how to respond. The person with the most flexibility will ensure keeping the communication flowing smoothly toward a successful resolution.

Further Considerations

As you learned in Chapter 1, all language is an attempt to persuade. With email, the more precise and to the point your message, the more favorably it will be received. Keeping it lean and mean will generate greater results and action. The following are essential considerations for making your email communications clearly understood.

This section demonstrates how information is best presented in email conversation. We all have a particular way we process that is unique to us. By recognizing the following distinctions, we can respond in a way that creates optimal understanding.

A. Create a clear and descriptive subject line. The language in the subject line should synopsize the information in the email clearly and compellingly before the email is opened and read.

B. Use an inverted information triangle. The fastest and most effective way to deliver information is from the top down. Use an inverted information triangle in your email communications by presenting the most important information first followed by information with descending levels of importance. People want to get to the important ideas and get to them fast in email. By doing this, you ensure the reader's attention is initially focused on what is most important and not lost in trivial or less important content. Readers have less time and more pressure. Give them what they want right up front.

Most important information
　Next most important information
　　Next most important information
　　　Least important information

C. Lean and mean active style. Creating messages that are clear and to the point makes it easier for the reader to understand and take action. Make every word used count. Long and wordy sentences will dilute your meaning and lose their impact. Provide all the necessary action items and time considerations for the situation at hand.

It is important to construct an action-oriented email to motivate the receiver. The use of "active voice" creates more dynamic and compelling emails, putting more energy into the message.

Example of active voice:

Passive: *It was felt that the presentation was too long.*
Active: *Jack thought the presentation was too long.*

Passive: *It has been decided by the CEO....*
Active: *The CEO decided....*

Passive: *It would be great to go to dinner.*
Active: *I am going to dinner.*

Chunk size–Sentence length. How much information is packed into and delivered in each sentence and the length of the sentence indicates how a person best processes information. Sentences can be short bullet style and packed with information or could be long and meandering. By responding in a similar style, they will identify more easily with your message.

Example:

Small Chunk Size:

The project was excellent. It was completed on time. The customer was satisfied.

Large Chunk Size:

The project was a great success and the people found it to be an exciting process. The schedule created was followed each week and the workers met their deadlines with customers from the West coast finding each phase beautifully finished and happy with the outcome.

It is important to recognize chunk size so you can match the way the sender takes in information. If you mismatch chunk size, it may reduce rapport and the ability for them to understand your response.

E. Spelling and punctuation. How you write says a lot about you. An email riddled with typos and grammar mistakes weakens the message, credibility, and impact of your message. Always use your email's spell checker and proofread your message before hitting the Send button. Simple mistakes can alter the reader's perception of you and your message.

F. Formal or informal communication. It is important to identify the sender's form of written communication. Is it a formal business style or casual approach? Maintain trust and rapport by matching the sender's email.

G. Focus on the recipient. Many times, in the heat of the workday, we can get confused as to what exactly our outcome is for the meeting we are in, the phone conversation we are having, and the email we are composing. It is important to be clear on your outcome. To do this, you must focus on what the receiver's interests are. You can then craft a message addressing their needs, concerns, and motivations. It is then and only then that you can truly create motivating and compelling messages. The more attentive you are to the concerns and communication style and manner of your customer, colleague or friends, the more clearly your message will be received.

Ask yourself the following questions before writing:

- Is this a formal or informal communication?
- How does the reader view me?
- What are their motivations, needs, or perspectives?
- What are their personal interests?
- Will the outcome impact them in a positive or negative way?
- What will they gain or lose?

When you step back and focus on what the reader truly desires, you can authentically enter their world. By asking yourself these questions, you will structure a compelling message centered on the reader's personal interests. Doors will open and actions will be taken.

H. Include previous key points when replying to an earlier message. Most people receive dozens of emails every day. Never assume that they will remember your previous exchange. Make it easy for them with a clear response.

It is challenging when someone sends you an email with answers you need but you cannot recall the original communication. This can be avoided by either simply adding in the original message when responding or refer to the key pieces of information that will help your reader.

I. Practice the 24-hour rule when your emotions are running high. During busy workdays, it is easy to overreact. This is not a good time to send an email. When your emotions are really engaged, it is best to use the 24-hour rule and wait until you are clear and calm before responding. Sending an email when emotionally charged can be a costly mistake. Cool off first before you hit the Send button.

J. When writing an email, visualize the person with whom you are communicating as if you were talking with them face to face.

Emoticons

Since the normal face-to-face cues of communication are missing in email, "emoticons" used in an appropriate context can fill an emotional void. The caveat to this is the *context* in which they are used. If it is a formal communication with someone with whom you are not very familiar, use your writing skills to create an appropriate emotional tone. In more casual and less formal communication, the use of emoticons is more appropriate.

The following are a few examples:

> The Wink ;-)
>   Demonstrates humor, a joke, or something sarcastic
>   "I know you will have fun tonight ;-)"

> The Smile :-)
>   Signifies happiness, humor, or fun
>   "The meeting was great today : -)"

> The Frown :-(
>   Indicates sadness or disappointment
>   "I wish we had seen John :-("

There are hundreds of emoticons used around the world. Appendix A has a comprehensive list of emoticons for your reference. Remember, as with many other techniques in this book, use emoticons in moderation. You do not want your message diluted and look unprofessional because of having plastered smiley faces all over your page.

Acronyms

The use of acronyms in email is common. Since we do not interpret many of them the same way, it is best to avoid using them. Acronyms also tend to create a more casual communication atmosphere. Here are a few common acronyms. (A more complete list appears in Appendix A.)

LOL	Lots of Love
LOL	Lots of laughs
CYA	See Ya
CYA	Cover Your Ass
FYI	For Your Information
FAQ	Frequently Asked Questions
CUL	See You Later

Salutations

Saying "hello" and "good-bye" is just as important in email communication as in a face-to-face meeting. It says, "I honor and respect you in this communication." Simply put, it shows you have "class." It is important to set a friendly tone with a respectful introduction, and to conclude with a positive and charming close.

Introductions
Hello
Hi
Good morning
Good afternoon
Good evening
Dear

Sign off's
Thanks
Thank you
Best/My Best
Regards/Best Regards
Have a great day/great afternoon/great evening
Sincerely
Respectfully

Legal Considerations

In today's litigious environment, it is important to understand that what you write is permanent and recorded. Email can be used as a legal document in a court of law. It seems every week there is another case of email records used as evidence. Be sure that what you write has no legal ramifications before you hit the Send button. This includes the areas of sexual harassment, slander, libel, and even plagiarism. So, make sure your emails are professional and respectful. If you are unsure as to what to include in an email, review the sections *Email When* and *Avoid Email When* in Chapter 1.

✔ Checklist

1. Identify the primary communication style of the sender
2. Identify key words in order to use Backtracking in your response
3. Identify the prevailing tone
4. Check for generalizing, deleting, distorting language
5. Identify Offset Words
6. Use benefit of the doubt and the Three Positions of Power

Action Item

Identify a situation where you would have liked to have responded more appropriately and effectively. Utilize the Three Positions of Power with this situation and see what new insights you gain through the process.

7

PUTTING IT ALL TOGETHER

"The difference between the right word and the almost right word is the difference between lightning and a lightning bug."

~ Mark Twain

As you develop your skills in deciphering the true message in your email conversations, it will become easy and automatic. You will know how to enter the world of your friend, customer, client, colleague, or employee. Using *The Language Response System,* you can respond in the most efficient manner creating the results you desire.

In this chapter, you will find some general considerations, practical steps, and *The Language Response System* checklist covering the skills and techniques you need for optimal and rewarding email communication. Depending on the time you have available and the importance of the email you are sending or receiving, you may choose to use one or all of the following steps in your response.

General Considerations

What is My Emotional State?

You've Got Mail! You have just received a message in your inbox. Even before you open the message, immediately identify the emotional state you are in. Do you feel clear, neutral, angry, calm, tired, or energized? By consciously acknowledging your own state of mind, you are in a position to send the most appropriate email or evaluate whether you are ready to receive the true message you've been sent. Fatigue, hunger, and stress all impact how you receive the email and how you choose to respond. If you are good to go, move on to the next step. If not, give yourself permission to take a break and come back to your email when you are in a more receptive and appropriate frame of mind.

What is the State of the Email and How Important is It?

Determine if the email is challenging or congenial. By ascertaining the overall tone and importance of the email, you can create an appropriate strategy to address the email at the onset of the communication.

What is My Outcome?

It is important to know what you want before responding to or initiating any email. Ask yourself, "What is my outcome?" "What do I want or not want?" Then, and only then, can you truly initiate or respond to an email with power. You must know your outcome to get what you want.

What Would Be the Best Method For Responding?

Is your impending conversation best handled by email? Perhaps a face-to-face meeting or phone call would be more appropriate.

The following is *The 60-Second Method* for quickly evaluating your emails. The four steps can be completed in 60 seconds providing insight for the right response. Chapter 8 will review the entire process as covered in this book, as well as cover some additional issues that may need to be addressed.

The 60-Second Method

Step 1: What communication style is being spoken?

Remember, there are two communication styles present in every email conversation: your's and the sender's. You will respond positively and unconsciously to the style that is similar to yours. Until you have integrated this, it is helpful to keep a reminder handy. Put a sticky note on your computer that says: "I am _____ " (fill in your style; VAKD). Now, determine what style the sender is using.

Evaluate the text for the communication style being presented (see Chapter 2 for more word choices in each category):

- Visual: see, look, picture
- Auditory: sounds good, hear, listen
- Kinesthetic: feels, texture, touch
- Digital: logical, think, order

Track the number of words used from each category. The frequency will give you a true indication of a particular communication style used by the sender. Anyone with a predominant communication style will repeatedly use language from that style.

Step 2: What is the tone and emotional temperature of the message?

What is the emotional disposition of the sender? (To become familiar with words that create tone, see Chapter 3). From the email, determine the prevailing tone: Imperative, Affirmative, Negative, or Tentative. Evaluate the message for key words and highlighted punctuation to see if the writer is agitated or calm. WORDS IN ALL CAPS are the same as shouting, so you will need to decide if the caps are to get your attention or to express anger or annoyance. Whatever the case, the writer wants you to take notice.

Step 3: Frequently used words – Backtracking

What words are frequently used? The words we use create a sense of connection and comfort for us, as well as reveal our values. Key words also let us know what is important to the person communicating with us. Make a note of the frequency of specific words that are used. You can then integrate (Backtrack) those key words in your response, which will create trust and rapport.

Step 4: What's the real message? Offset Words.

Understanding the real message is what we're interested in. Consciously, we use Offset Words to transition a phrase – to unconsciously deliver a message. The truth of the message usually comes after the Offset word is used. If the sender has used an Offset word, identify any incongruence that has been created. For example, "Your report was excellent, *but* we are not going to use your suggestions." What is the real message? Remember: The unconscious mind always wants to tell the truth.

Common Offset Words:
- But
- However
- Nonetheless
- Nevertheless
- Anyway
- Yet

The 60-Second Method Checklist

Steps	Your Position	The Sender
1: VAKD What sensory communication style is present?	Visual Auditory Kinesthetic Digital	Visual Auditory Kinesthetic Digital
2: Tone What is the tone of the email, neutral or....?	Imperative Affirmative Negative Tentative	Imperative Affirmative Negative Tentative
3: Backtracking What words do they use?		Words 1. 2. 3.
4: Offset Words Did the sender use an Offset Word? Yes No		But, Yet, However (What is the real meaning?)

Depending on the level of importance and outcome of the communication, you may choose to evaluate the email even further. If you find your emotions running high or you're just not sure what the real message is, "benefit of the doubt" and the Three Positions of Power are always valuable for ensuring clear communication.

The 60-Second Method approach is a sure method for quickly assessing any email and crafting an appropriate response. And, as with all things, knowing the basics inside and out will always provide you with a skill set that will stand you in good stead throughout your life. Chapter 8 will provide a complete checklist of *The Language Response System* so you are always prepared.

8

HERE'S A REVIEW

*"Do not dwell in the past, do not dream
of the future, concentrate the mind
on the present moment."*

~ Buddha

I n our world of ever-increasing technology, the ability to communicate with effectiveness and clarity is essential. Technology is continually speeding things up. In spite of the speed of the digital world, if you want to be understood, you must create the human connection with each and every person with whom you communicate. Essentially, our ultimate goal is to be understood. When this happens, we feel accepted and ultimately respected. By taking the time to tune in and utilize the components of *The Language Response System*, you will be able to transform your email conversations into positive outcomes. By mastering this formidable process, you can reconnect, revitalize your communications, and create the results you desire.

Chapter 7 outlined *The 60-Second Method*. This chapter provides a complete checklist of *The Language Response System* and includes a number of examples. Additionally, you'll find some final do's and don'ts to ensure that your email communications are professional, engaging, and ultimately rewarding.

The Complete *Language Response System* Checklist

- **Emotional position and intended outcome:** What is your current emotion and disposition? Are you calm and clear? If not, determine if this has anything to do with the email you received and create a calm environment before responding. If you open your email and find it is a hot topic, wait a couple of hours or until the next day and then review it. What is the importance level of the communication? Know what outcome you desire before replying. Make sure it is clear. Be positive, upbeat, and charming.

- Is the email conversation about a problem or is it conveying a state of contentment? What is the level of importance?

- What is your outcome in responding?

- What would be the best method for responding?

1. Identify the primary communication style of the sender	Visual, Auditory, Kinesthetic, Digital?
2. Identify key words in order to use Backtracking in your response	Backtracking: What familiar words does the sender use that would create rapport for them?
3. Identify the prevailing tone	What key words is the sender using and what emotional position is indicated?
4. Check for generalizing, deleting, distorting language	Is the sender over-generalizing, deleting, and/or distorting? Are they using vague and ambiguous language? Is the sender associated or dissociated to the content of the email conversation, i.e., connected or disconnected?
5. Identify Offset Words	Identify the Offset Words and what they are negating in the email conversation. Determine where the conversation is congruent and in alignment – and where it is not.
6. Use benefit of the doubt and the Three Positions of Power	Use benefit of the doubt with information that is emotional, controversial or unclear, "as if you don't have all the information." Three Positions of Power: Shift yourself into the position of your shoes, their shoes, and as a detached observer. Utilize the insight you gain and learn from each position.

When you've completed the six steps of *The Language Response System*, there are three more areas to consider before sending your email response.

A. **Legalities:** Are there legal implications with the message? If so, take care.

B. **Passage of Time:** What action or inaction has taken place between email conversations?

C. **Re-read:** Re-read emails before sending. Check punctuation, spelling, and tone. If you feel charged about the topic, save the email in your Drafts folder and come back to it later.

The most important of these last three steps involves being sensible and prudent in your email communication. Essentially, it's the same as when we were young and an adult suggested that you should think before you speak. I'm sure you can think of a time when you said something you regretted as soon as you said it. We've all been there. At least with email conversations, we have the option of responding in a thoughtful manner before clicking the Send button. A final reading also allows us the chance to take a deep breath and calmly focus ourselves to ensure that what needs to be conveyed in our email is what will help our relationship continue to grow to the benefit of all parties. With that in mind, there are a few things we need to be mindful of avoiding when dealing with email.

Depending on the level of importance of the communication and outcome, you may choose to evaluate the email even further. If you find your emotions running high or you're just not sure what the real message is, using "benefit of the doubt" and the Three Positions of Power is always a good idea. The following are further steps in evaluating an email.

Benefit of the Doubt

Things are not always as they seem. Become a master at giving the benefit of the doubt and you will create a new reality for yourself. The world travels at light speed, makes assumptions too quickly and jumps to conclusions, often to our detriment. By using the benefit of the doubt, you create a safe space for others to be authentic with you. Always take the position of giving the other person or persons the benefit of the doubt.

Create a practice that separates you from the message, regardless of its content. Ask yourself:

1. "What could be going on here?"
2. "What don't I know?"
3. "What could I be missing?"

Three Positions of Power – Put Yourself in Their Shoes

The person with the greatest flexibility in viewing a situation from multiple positions has the most powerful communication. You are in control. To get to the possible truth of a message, use the Three Positions of Power to gain clarity and understanding.

- Read the email in your shoes.
- Read the email in their shoes.
- Read the email as a neutral observer.

Position of Speaking

What is the sender's position of speaking: Are they associated or dissociated? How does their position influence the content? Are they connected to the situation or are they detached? Use these clues to evaluate the current emotional state of the writer. Knowing their state will help you create an effective response.

Navigate the Emotional Terrain – Plan Your Response

The general disposition of email will give you a sense of the emotional state of the writer. Knowing if they are happy or sad, frustrated or calm will let you know the environment in which your message will be received. We all know that our emotions change quickly. If you know the writer, does the tone appear to be consistent with who you know them to be? In this step, integrate any additional information that would assist you in assessing the email: previous phone calls, meetings, etc.

The following pages provide examples using
The Language Response System email checklist.

Example 1

Laura,

I am *looking* for a new home. Are there any listings I can *see* in the *South Shore*? Steven referred me to you; he said you know how to *spot* a *great* deal. I am very interested in *seeing* something.

See you soon,
Vince

Email Evaluation

Vince is interested in finding a new home. His emotional state is neutral with a high level of importance. He is communicating Visually: his tone is neutral and he is speaking in an associated way using "I" showing that he is connected to the content of his email. Key words he uses are: *Great* and *South Shore*.

1. Emotional state: Neutral
2. Importance level: High
3. Sensory style: Visual (looking, see, seeing, spot)
4. Tone and position of speaking: Neutral, associated
5. Key words and phrases: Great, South Shore
6. No Offset Words

Email Response

Vince,

I appreciate your contacting me and your interest. I would love to *show* you two of the listings I have. They both *look* great and are on the *South Shore*.

My Best,
Laura

Review of the Response:

- Laura's response starts with the use of the agreement frame, "I appreciate," to show gratitude, which starts the conversation off on the right foot.

- Her response incorporates Vince's sensory language – *show* and *look* – to connect to Vince's style and the best way he takes in information.

- Using Backtracking, Laura integrates the following words – *great* and *South Shore* – so that Vince feels the connection consciously and unconsciously.

Example 2

> GT auto dealer,
> I am shopping for a new GT. I have *heard* that it's an *amazing* car. It *sounds* like it has been very *popular* with the people who have them. Could you give me a *call* to *discuss* the *options*?
>
> Regards,
> Jim

Email Evaluation

Jim is interested in a new car, his emotional state and importance level are high. His communication style is Auditory, his tone neutral, and he is speaking in an associated way using "I" showing that he is connected to the content of his email. Key words he uses are: *Popular, options, amazing*.

1. Emotional state: High
2. Importance level: High
3. Sensory style: Auditory (heard, sounds, call, discuss)
4. Tone and position of speaking: Neutral, associated
5. Key words and phrases: Popular, options, amazing

Email Response

> Jim,
> We appreciate your *inquiry* and we would love to *tell* you all about the GT. Yes, it has been *popular* and people have been *amazed* by its performance and reliability. They have really been *talking* it up. When is the best time to reach you so we can *discuss* the *options*?
>
> *Talk* with you soon,
> David

Review of the Response:

- David's response begins with the use of the agreement frame, "I appreciate," to acknowledge Jim's interest.

- He uses Jim's sensory language – *inquiry, tell, talking,* and *discuss* – to connect to his style and how he best takes in information.

- Using Backtracking, David integrates his key words – *popular, amazed, options* – to create comfort and connection both consciously and unconsciously.

Example 3

> Randy,
> I am *thinking about* finding a new broker and *need* to know what your *thoughts* are on the market. Determination is how I have made my money and I am *considering* you to be on my *team*.
> I am *thinking about* making a shift soon. Give me a call.
>
> Thanks,
> Jeff

Email Evaluation

Jeff's emotional position is high and his level of importance is also high. He is communicating from the Digital style, his tone is Imperative (he "needs to"). He is communicating from an associated position demonstrating his personal connection to the email content. His keywords: *Determination* and *Team.*

1. Emotional state: High
2. Importance level: High
3. Sensory Style: Digital (think, know, thought)
4. Tone and position of speaking: Imperative (need to), associated
5. Key words and phrases: Determination, team
6. Apply: 3 Positions of Power

Email Response

> Jeff,
> Thanks for your interest in our firm. I *think* you will appreciate our *logic* and how we *think* about investments in this new market. I invite you to our offices so you can *learn* about our *team*. Our firm is *determined* to provide the best service for you.
>
> My Best,
> Randy

Review of the Response:

- Randy's response begins with "Thanks" to acknowledge Jeff's interest and to start off on the right foot.

- He uses Jeff's Digital sensory language – *think, logic,* and *learn* – to connect to his style and how he best takes in information.

- Using Backtracking, Randy integrates Jeff's key words – *team* and *determination* – to create comfort and a familiar atmosphere.

- Randy's response uses the appropriate tone to add urgency.

Example 4

Brian,

I am *not* sure what your requirements are of me. I *feel* you are *not comfortable* with my *expertise*. It *might be* good just to talk over what you *could* want from me in my *role. Could* we get together to *feel* out the best use of my *expertise*? I have *done* my best and it *does not* seem to matter. I like *working* on the *team*, however, I am *not being* utilized.

Thank you,
Cindy

Email Evaluation

Cindy is concerned about her job. Her emotional position is high and importance is high. She communicates from the Kinesthetic style. The tone of the email is Tentative and negative. She is speaking from the associated position demonstrating her connection to the issue. Her key words are: *Expertise, I feel, role,* and *team.* By identifying the Offset word "however," we see the true meaning within the message in which she feels underutilized.

1. Emotional state: High
2. Importance level: High
3. Sensory style: Kinesthetic (I feel, comfortable, get, done, working, being)
4. Tone and position of speaking: Tentative (might, could) and negative (not), associated
5. Key words and phrases: Expertise, I feel, role, team
6. Offset Words: However
7. Apply: Benefit of the doubt and the Three Positions of Power

Email Response

> Cindy,
>
> I *appreciate* your *expressing* how you *feel* and your *expertise* is important to the project. Each *team* member has their role and your *role* will *play* a more significant part in phase two of the project. I am available this Friday to *get connected* on exactly what your responsibilities are so you and I will be *on the same page*. I am committed that you do *feel* part of the *team* and I want to *utilize* your full talents on this project.
>
> Regards,
> Brian

Review of the Response:

- Brian's response begins with use of the agreement frame, "I appreciate," to calm and neutralize the situation.

- He uses Cindy's sensory language – *feel, same page, will play,* and *stronger* – to connect to her style and how she best takes in information.

- Using Backtracking, Brian integrates Cindy's key words – *feel, expertise, team, role, talk over,* and *utilize* – to create comfort and a familiar atmosphere.

- Brian's response uses the appropriate tone for her emotional state and addresses the concerns of her email.

Example 5

> ABC shoes,
> I have been a *customer* for two years. I *can't* understand, *looking* at these shoes, how they fell apart. I *see* that *I have to look* for another brand. What *value* did I get for my *money*? *Looking cool* is important *but* not more than *losing money* on a *bad* purchase. *I can't* believe how fast they wore out.
>
> Your *customer*,
> Anthony Jackson

Email Evaluation

Anthony is upset about the lack of quality and durability of his shoes. The emotional state and importance level are both high. He communicates from the Visual style. His tone is Imperative, negative, and he is communicating from an associated position indicating his connection to this issue. Key words he uses are: *customer, money, looking cool,* and *value.*

1. Emotional state: High
2. Importance level: High, problem
3. Sensory style: Visual (see, looking)
4. Tone and position of speaking: Imperative (I can't) and negative, associated
5. Keywords and phrases: Customer, money, looking cool, value
6. Offset Words: But
7. Apply: Benefit of the doubt and the Three Positions of Power

Email Response

> Mr. Jackson,
> *Thank you* for contacting ABC shoes. *Reviewing* your situation, we can *see* that they did not perform as you expected. We are committed to your *looking cool* and also getting your *money's* worth. ABC stands behind its product and its *customers*. We are shipping you a new pair today. Enjoy the new shoes.
>
> Thank You,
> ABC Shoes

Review of the Response:

- ABC's response begins with an appropriate positive tone knowing Mr. Jackson's emotions are high and negative.

- ABC Shoes uses Mr. Jackson's sensory language – *reviewing, see,* and *look* – to connect to his style and how he best takes in information.

- Using Backtracking, the following words are integrated – *looking cool, money,* and *customer* – to create comfort and a familiar atmosphere for Mr. Jackson.

The previous examples demonstrate how *The Language Response System* helps you to thoroughly evaluate and effectively respond to email communiqués. How much evaluation time you apply to any email is determined by its level of importance. To ensure that your emails create the outcome you intend, the following do's and don'ts will give you the final edge.

Email Etiquette: Do's and Don'ts

1. **Avoid humor and sarcasm:** Email conversation lacks the "live" component of tone and verbal modulation. The humor and sarcasm of your conversation can easily be misunderstood.

2. **Use correct punctuation and grammar:** Look professional by using correct grammar and punctuation.

3. **Use precision language:** Use language that is specific and to the point.

4. **Inverted triangle:** Give the most important information first, followed by the next important and so on. If a person is short on time, they will get the essence of your message quickly.

5. **Active voice:** Use active voice and verb tense when appropriate. Active voice creates movement and doesn't put things somewhere in the future.

6. **Respond as if you where face to face with your conversation partner:** Picture the person you are emailing as you respond. Write the conversation as if you were with them in person.

7. **Respond in a positive, upbeat and charming manner.** Your mother was right; you will attract more flies with honey than with vinegar.

8. **Appreciation frame.** Let people know what you appreciate and are committed to, and take a stance that provides confidence and honors their world.

9. **Be your word, do what you say.** Your reputation is hard to develop and easily destroyed.

10. **Respond without emotion.** Keep emotion out of your email conversation. Avoid using all caps, bold type, and any other modifications of text that might mistakenly convey unintended emotion.

Some Final Thoughts

We are living in challenging times. Communication, now more then ever, is of paramount importance. *The Language Response System* is a powerful toolset that helps you create and maintain rewarding relationships. No matter what your situation is or the content of an email you receive, you now know the fundamental challenges of email communication and have the skills to respond in an engaging, compelling and powerful manner.

Every email you receive is from another person and, just like you, they have the same challenge before them: being human. Every challenge you are presented with is a chance to take yourself to a whole new level of understanding: understanding yourself and the world around you. The more skills you gain to aid you in this process, the more satisfaction you'll feel within yourself. Life will take on a new sheen of interest and depth.

As was stated in Chapter 1, "Language is the currency of our lives and the words we choose shape our reality. They are the map to our beliefs, values, emotions, and personality. It is the choice and manner in which we write that gives us the clues to what is happening in our world." Each of us has the ability to create an extraordinary world. By using *The Language Response System* and keeping your cool, you will master the number one form of business communication – email.

"Watch your thoughts; they become your words.
Watch your words; they become your actions.
Watch your actions; they become your habits.
Watch your habits; they become your character.
Watch your character for it will become your destiny."

~ Frank Outlaw

Appendix A:

Acronyms, Common Email Symbols, and Emoticons

As with any culture, the electronic world has a vibration and a language of its own. This appendix will keep you up-to-date with the prevailing code in email.

Acronym	Definition
$0.02	My two cents
AAMOF	As a matter of fact
ADN	Any day now
AFAIK	As far as I know
AFK	Away from keyboard
ASAP	As soon as possible
A/S	Age/ sex
A/S/L	Age/ sex/ location
AYSOS	Are you stupid or something?
BIAB	Back in a bit
BBL	Be back later
BCC	Blind carbon copy
BCNU	Be seeing you
BF	Boyfriend
BFD	Big freakin' deal
BFN	Bye for now
BG	Big girl
BION	Believe it or not
BTSOOM	Beats the {stuffing} out of me
BTDT	Been there, done that
BTW	By the way
BRB	Be right back
BWDIK	But what do I know?
BYAM	Between you and me
BYKT	But you knew that

Acronym	Definition
CC	Carbon copy
C4N	Ciao for now
CMIIW	Correct me if I'm wrong
CU	See you
CUA	Commonly used acronyms or common user access
CUL, CUL8R	See you later
CULA	See you later alligator
CWOT	Complete waste of time
CYA	See ya
DARFC	Ducking and running for cover
DHYB	Don't hold your breath
DIIK	Darned if I know
DOB	Date of birth
F2F	Face to face
FAQ	Frequently asked questions
FBOW	For better or worse
FITB	Fill in the blank
FU	Fouled up
FUBAR	Fouled up beyond recognition
FUD	{spreading} Fear, uncertainty, and disinformation
FWIW	For what it's worth
FYA	For your amusement
FYI	For your information
FYM	For your misinformation
G	Grin
GBU	God bless you
GD&R	Grinning, ducking, and running
GD&RF	Grinning, ducking, and running fast
GD&W	Grinning, ducking, and weaving
GF	Girl friend

Acronym	Definition
GFETE	Grinning from ear to ear
GG	Good game or Gotta go
GIGO	Garbage in, Garbage out
GJ	Good job
GL	Good luck
GMTA	Great minds think alike
HAK	Hugs and kisses
HHOK	Ha-Ha, Only kidding
HHOS	Ha-Ha, Only serious
HTH	Hope this helps
IAC	In any case
IAE	In any event
IANAL	I am not a lawyer
IANAMD	I am not a doctor
IBTD	I beg to differ
IC	I see
IDK or IDN	I don't know
ILY	I love you
IMCO	In my considered opinion
IME	In my experience
IMHO	In my humble opinion
IMNSHO	In my not-so-humble opinion
IMO	In my opinion
IMPE	In my personal experience
INPO	In no particular order
IOW	In other words
IRL	In real life
ISWYM	I see what you mean
IWALU	I will always love you
IYKWIM	If you know what I mean
J/K	Just kidding

Acronym	Definition
JAS	Just a second
JFF	Just for fun
JIC	Just in case
JTLYK	Just to let you know
K	Okay
KISS	Keep it simple, stupid
KIT	Keep in touch
KMA	Kiss my ass
KWIM	Know what I mean?
KYFC	Keep your fingers crossed
L	Laugh
LOL	Laughing out loud, lot's of laughter, lot's of luck, lot's of love
LTHTT	Laughing too hard to type
MGB	May God bless
MHOTY	My hat's off to you
MOTAS	Member of the appropriate sex
MOTD	Message of the day
MOTOS	Member of the opposite sex
MOTSS	Member of the same sex
MTFBWY	May the force be with you
MYOB	Mind your own business
NBD	No big deal
NC	No comment
NFW	No freakin' way
NOYB	None of your business
NRN	No reply necessary
NTIM	Not that it matters
NTW	Not to worry
NTYMI	Now that you mention it
OBTW	Oh, by the way
OIC	Oh, I see

Acronym	Definition
OMG	Oh my God!
OMIK	Open mouth, insert key
ONNA	Oh no, not again
OOTB	Out of the Box (brand new)
OS	Operating system
OTFL	On the floor laughing
OTL	Out to lunch
OTOH	On the other hand
OTOOH	On the "other" other hand
OTTH	On the third hand
PAW	Parents are watching
PC	Personal computer or politically correct
PITA	Pain in the ass
PMFJI	Pardon me for jumping in
POS	Parents over shoulder
POSSLQ	Person of the opposite sex sharing living quarters
POV	Point of view
RBTL	Read between the lines
RL	Real life
ROTFL	Rolling on the floor laughing
ROTFLASTC	Rolling on the floor laughing and scaring the cat
ROTFLMAO	Rolling on the floor laughing my ass off
RSN	Real soon now
RTBM	Read the bloody manual
RTFAQ	Read the frequently asked questions
RTFM	Read the freakin' manual
RTM	Read the manual
SCNR	Sorry, could not resist
SITD	Still in the dark

Acronym	Definition
SNAFU	Situation normal, all fouled up
SO	Significant other
SWAK	Sealed with a kiss
SITD	Still in the dark
SYS	See you soon
TANSTAAFL	There ain't no such thing as a free lunch
TEOTWAWKI	The end of the world as we know it
TFTT	Thanks for the thought
TGAL	Think globally, act locally
THX, TX	Thanks
TIA	Thanks in advance
TIC	Tongue in cheek
TLA	Three-letter acronym
TMI	Too much information
TOBAL	There ought to be a law
TOBG	This ought to be good
TOS	Terms of service
TPTB	The powers that be
TTBOMK	To the best of my knowledge
TTFN	Ta-ta for now
TTYL	Talk to you later
TTYT	Talk to you tomorrow
TY	Thank you
TYVM	Thank you very much
VBG	Very big grin
WB	Welcome back
WMMOWS	Wash my mouth out with soap
WRT	With respect to
WTB	Want to buy
WTF	What the f—?
WTG	Way to go!
WWW	World wide web

Acronym	Definition
WYGIWYPF	What you get is what you pay for
WYSIWYG	What you see is what you get
YABA	Yet another bloody acronym
YGIAGAM	Your guess is as good as mine
YGLT	You're gonna love this
YKYA_W	You know you're a (fill in the blank) when
YMMV	Your mileage may vary
YNK	You never know
YW	You're welcome
YYSW	Yeah, yeah, sure, whatever
7/24	All day long, seven days a week, 24 hours a day

Common Email Symbols & Emoticons

Symbol	Definition	Symbol	Definition
_ : -) or :)	Smile, happy	_ : -(or : (	Unhappy
;-)	Wink, jest	I -O	Yawning
: -))	Very happy	=)	Surprised
:-D	Laughing	:-O	Shocked
:-<	Forlorn	;'-C	Crying
:-e	Disappointed	>:-<	Mad
>:- (	Mad	(:-<	Frowning
(:- (	Frowning	:->	Sarcastic
:-p	Sticking tongue out	:-*	Kiss
d:-o	Taking one's hat off to a great idea	;-8	Talking out both sides of one's mouth
;-y	Saying it with a smile	:-v	Is talking
:-V	Shouting	: -(0)	Yelling
*:-I	Daydreaming	:-{	Someone with a mustache
=^..^=	Cat	:-}	Nervous smile
:o}	Bashful/embarrassed	:o[	Not impressed
8-)	Wearing glasses	:-)8	Wearing a bow tie
B-)	Wearing sunglasses	=: O	WOW
=o)	Pleasant surprise	:-x	My lips are sealed
};-)>	Devil	O:-)	Angel
:q	Licking upper lip	: -)}	Trying not to laugh
:-/	Grim	{{{}}}	Lots of hugs
:-&	Tongue tied	$-)	Greedy
X-)	I saw nothing	:-I	Indifferent
(-:	Happy left-hander	:-7	Wry comment
:-S	Confused	:-c	Depressed
OOo:-)	Thinking	:( )=	Can't stop talking

Appendix B:

Learning Tool Cutouts

Email Checklist

Steps	Your Position	The Sender
Step 1: What is my emotional state?	Low Neutral High	Low Neutral High
What is the importance level of the communication?	Low Neutral High	Low Neutral High
Step 2: Is the email a problem, desired, or neutral state?	Problem Desired Neutral	Problem Desired Neutral
Step 3: What sensory communication style is present?	Visual Auditory Kinesthetic Digital	Visual Auditory Kinesthetic Digital
Step 4: What is the tone of the email?	Imperative Affirmative Negative Tentative	Imperative Affirmative Negative Tentative
Check for over- generalizing, deleting, and distorting		Is the sender over- generalizing, deleting, and/or distorting? Are they using vague and ambiguous language?

Steps	Your Position	The Sender
Check for associated or dissociated language		Is the sender connected or disconnected from the content of the email?
Step 5: Backtracking What words are they using?		Words 1. 2. 3.
Step 6: Do they use Offset Words? Yes No		But Yet However
Step 7: Should you use benefit of the doubt?	How could I have misread this situation?	What could be going on? What emotions are present: Fear, doubt, isolation, confusion, etc.?
Step 8: Three Positions of Power	Your Shoes:	Their Shoes: Neutral Party
Step 9: Plan your response using Steps 1-7	Most important issue to you.	Most important issue to them.

The 60-Second Method Checklist

Steps	Your Position	The Sender
1: VAKD What sensory communication style is present?	Visual Auditory Kinesthetic Digital	Visual Auditory Kinesthetic Digital
2: Tone What is the tone of the email?	Imperative Affirmative Negative Tentative	Imperative Affirmative Negative Tentative
3: Backtracking What words do they use?		Words 1. 2. 3.
4: Offset Words Did the sender use an Offset Word? Yes No		But, Yet, However (What is the real meaning?)

Primary Communication Styles

Visual	Auditory	Kinesthetic	Digital
Clear	Hear	Feel	Think
View	Tell	Touch	Concrete
Imagine	Speak	Hold	Learn
Sight	Talk	Grasp	Understand
Picture	Sounds	Walk	Thoughts
See	Voice	Soft	Consider
Look	Question	Smooth	Logic
Focus	Heard	Strong	Sense
Read	Listen	Calm	Decide
Highlight	Call	Handle	Process
Clarify	Inquire	Concrete	Distinct
Reveal	Tone	Dry	Study
Show	Resonate	Felt	Perceive

The Agreement Frame

Neutralize	Calm	Control
I Appreciate	Views	And
I respect	Saying	
I agree with your	Feelings	
	Thoughts	
	Ideas	
	Opinions	

Bibliography

Angell, David and Brent Heslop. *The Elements of Email Style: Communicate Effectively via Electronic Mail.* New York: Addison-Wesley, 1994.

Bailey, Keith and Leland, Karen. *Online Customer Service for Dummies.* New York, NY: Hungry Minds, Inc., 2001.

Baker, Kim and Sunny. *How to Say It Online.* Paramus, NJ: Prentice Hall Press, 2001.

Baron, Naomi S. *Alphabet to Email: How Written English Evolved and Where It's Heading.* New York, NY: Routledge, 2000.

Buckingham, Marcus and Coffman, Curt. *First, Break All the Rules.* New York, NY: Simon and Schuster, 1999.

De Rodriguez, Gary. *Master Your Destiny.* San Diego, CA. The Neuro-Linguistic Training Center of San Diego, 1998.

Flynn, Nancy and Tom. *Writing Effective Email.* Menlo Park, CA: Crisp Publications, 1998.

Haden-Elgin, Suzette. *The Gentle Art of Written Self-Defense: How to Write Your Way Out of Life's Delicate Situations.* New York, NY: MJF Books, 1993.

Haden-Elgin, Suzette. *The Gentle Art of Verbal Self-Defense at Work.* Paramus, NJ: Prentice Hall Press, 2000.

Hall, L. Michael and Bodenhamer, Bob G. *Figuring Out People: Design Engineering With Meta-Programs.* United Kingdom: Crown House Publishing Limited, 1997.

Bodenhamer, Bob G., and Hall, L. Michael. *The User's Manual For The Brain.* United Kingdom: The Cromwell Press, 2000.

Hogan, Kevin. *The Science of Influence: How to Get Anyone to Say Yes in 8 Minutes or Less.* Hoboken, NJ: John Wiley and Sons, Inc., 2005.

Horn, Sam. *Tongue Fu! How To Deflect, Disarm, and Defuse Any Verbal Conflict.* New York, NY: St. Martin's Griffin, 1996.

Knight, Sue. *NLP at Work: Neuro Linguistic Programming, The Difference that Makes a Difference in Business.* London: Nicholas Brealey Publishing, 1995.

Locke, John L. *Why We Don't Talk to Each Other Anymore: The De-Voicing of Society.* New York, NY: Touchstone, 1998.

Rose-Charvet, Shelle. *Words That Change Minds: Mastering the Language of Influence.* Dubuque, Iowa: Kendall/Hunt Publishing Company, 1995.

Pease Allen and Barbara, *Why Men Don't Listen and Women Can't Read Maps.* UK: Orion, 2001.

About the Author

Steven Griffith, president of Steven Griffith & Associates, is a language and communications specialist and performance coach. A certified trainer in Neuro Linguistic Programming Griffith coaches executives, professional athletes and celebrities, how to maximize their productivity through the effective use of written and spoken language.

Griffith's *Language Response System*™, has been used effectively by major organizations around the world including Citibank, ADP, Wells Fargo, Coldwell Banker, and the LAPD. He is the creator of *Intelligent Mail*, the world's first software program that evaluates email communication and coaches the user how best to respond. He has been featured on national television and radio as a communication and performance coach.

Steven spends most of his time training companies and individuals how to leverage business communication for maximum advantage and how to identify and overcome the barriers that impede performance.

A former Golden Glove boxer and football player, Griffith lives in Southern California.

For more information about coaching and training, contact Steven at www.emailpower.com